ANGLING FOR WORDS

Study Book

Carolyn C. Bowen

Decoding and Spelling Practice

Academic Therapy Publications
Novato, California

HOW TO USE THIS READING STUDY BOOK
Follow the Fish!

1. Present each letter in a multisensory manner. Follow the letter order shown on the index before each level. Place reading and spelling cards that have been introduced in separate stacks for daily review.* (A complete list of reading and spelling responses are listed in the companion ANGLING FOR WORDS WORKBOOK.)

2. Give auditory practice of sound for recognition in initial, medial, and final positions in words. (t) tap water faucet

3. Read part or all of the words on a page listed under that letter. These words contain ONLY those letters previously presented.

4. If a fish appears on right, refer to that page for pertinent exercise in companion ANGLING FOR WORDS WORKBOOK. If a fish appears on left, however, the exercise referred to would be helpful before reading word lists.

5. It is recommended that each student keep a loose-leaf notebook with the following sections in it:

   1. Basewords   4. Plurals and Possessives
   2. Syllable Division   5. Learned Words
   3. Affixes   6. Other

   As both sides of an exercise sheet are completed, the student transfers the page to his own notebook. Within each section, he groups exercises containing like concepts. This process of organizing material into appropriate categories is particularly helpful in developing a mental organization of rules and principles of reading and spelling.

6. Exaggerated pronunciation of short vowels, distinct from casual running speech, is an absolute necessity for the language student and serves as a spelling aid. Examples: label, table; in ci dent, prec e dent. Particular care must also be taken in pronouncing sounds such as (d) and (p), NOT (duh) and (puh). r and l should not become (ur) and (ul). Again, for spelling clarity, avoid the schwa in sound pictures to represent the vowel in unaccented syllables. Example: (dis tănt) NOT (dis tənt).

7. In this program basewords, sometimes called roots in other books, refer to the complete words to which affixes can be added. The first six levels deal with the reading and spelling of basewords, plus suffixes which can be added without changing the baseword spelling. Level VII deals with spelling rules for adding suffixes and for forming plurals and possessives.

8. Abbreviations used are: b.w. = baseword; syl. = syllable; C and con. = consonant; V. = vowel; suf. = suffix; L.W. = learned word.

*9. For teachers who have not had training in multisensory presentations, ANGLING FOR WORDS – THE TEACHER'S LINE, Dorothy B. Montgomery, Academic Therapy Publications, presents the program as used in public school resource rooms. ANGLING PHONO-CARDS for reading and spelling are also available.

INTRODUCTION

<u>Background</u>

This study book was developed in the Summer Language Training Program at the Hockaday School, Dallas, Texas, by language therapists trained in the Orton-Gillingham approach as taught in the Language Training Unit of the Neurology Division of Texas Scottish Rite Hospital, Dallas, Lucius Waites, M.D., Director.

The program has been used with individual students and in small classes of elementary through high school grades. The purpose of the program is to teach the language as IT is to the child as HE is. By over-learning the reliable principles of reading and spelling, the student eventually begins to substitute reasoning for guessing. The presentation presumes nothing on the part of the student except average intellectual ability. It <u>does</u> assume thorough training on the part of the therapist in a multisensory, structured, and sequential approach to the language.

<u>Sequence</u>

It is important that the concepts outlined here be presented sequentially; however, levels are interchangeable if words which involve unpresented concepts are omitted. The amount of drill necessary to develop each concept must be determined by the student's age, ability, and degree of disability. Anna Gillingham believed a student should go as fast as he can and as slow as he must. The lists, as well as the inserted reading matter, provide continuous daily review of letters and concepts. A lesson plan should involve a review of all reading and spelling cards which have been presented, <u>reading</u> columns from several different lists (perhaps one new, four review), cursive <u>writing</u>, and <u>spelling</u> dictations. Much chanting of rules and constant review and repetition are strongly suggested.

<u>Structure and Terminology</u>

1. Nonsense words and unusual real words are used to challenge the phonetic skills of the reader. Asterisks (**) denote made-up nonsense words which follow regular reading or spelling rules.

2. When a word uses the second (less common) sound of a digraph, the digraph is underlined once; the third sound has two underlines. (chair, <u>Christmas</u>, <u><u>chef</u></u>; easel, he<u>a</u>d, ste<u>a</u>k.)

3. Primary type with serifs is used for better visual discrimination.

4. The pages in the Workbook labeled Reading Cards and Spelling Cards represent the most frequent or regularly used responses for reading and spelling. In the text and workbook, <u>underlines</u> denote letter names; ( ) indicate sounds.

5. Situation (or generalization) pages in the Workbook help the student to learn to spell a particular sound in its various positions – initial, medial, and final. The therapist should dictate a few regularly-spelled words at a time, allowing the student to choose the proper column. See p. 11 in Workbook, Situation Summary.

6. Above each story are the words which do not follow the regular rules for reading. They need to be presented before reading with their irregularities noted.

7. Simplified DEFINITIONS as related to Language Training

VOWEL – letter with an open sound   CONSONANT – a letter with blocked or partially-blocked sound

VOICED AND UNVOICED PARTNERS: Letters whose sounds are formed by the same mouth position. The sounds differ only because of the absence or use of vocal cords.

voiced - unvoiced	voiced - unvoiced	voiced - unvoiced
(j) - (ch)	(d) - (t)	(g) - (k)
(z) - (s)	(b) - (p)	(v) - (f)
(zh) - (sh)		

INITIAL – first   MEDIAL – middle (any position but first or last)

FINAL – last

SYLLABLE - a word or part of word made by one voice impulse; has one V sound

OPEN SYL. – ends in vowel   CLOSED SYL. – ends in consonant

REGULAR – most common   IRREGULAR – less common

LEARNED WORDS – words that do not follow the regular patterns for reading or spelling.

KEY WORDS – words which "unlock" the sounds of letters

NONSENSE WORDS – made-up words which are phonetic and follow the rules of Eng.

BASE WORDS – complete words

SUFFIX – a letter or group of letters added to the end of a baseword to change its use in a sentence

PREFIX – a letter or group of letters added to the beginning of a baseword to change its meaning

Acknowledgments

1. References for word lists and diacritical markings are based on Webster's New International Dictionary 2nd edition. Exceptions are listed on the index pages of Level II.
2. Procedures for the therapists are based on the publications of Aylett R. Cox, Associate Director of the Language Training Unit of Texas Scottish Rite Hospital: Structure and Techniques, Remedial Language Training; Situation Reading; and Situation Spelling, an outgrowth of the Fifth Edition of the Gillingham-Stillman manual, Remedial Training. These materials were originally published by Educators Publishing Service, 31 Smith Place, Cambridge, MA 02138.
3. Alice Koontz is responsible for the book's overall design, original materials, organization and art work. Margaret Adair initiated and inspired the first efforts of compilation. Ann Harris and Judy Dusek have done the typing and proofreading. Without the willing and enthusiastic labors of my faithful husband, Dub, this book would not have been possible. Particular thanks go to all our students in language therapy who have been patient in learning with us the intricacies of our language. Perhaps this work can help save a few Anglers from the Sea of Look-Say.

Carolyn C. Bowen, Dallas, Texas

CONCEPTS

One-syl. words are arranged in following order up to the presentation of letter <u>u</u>:

1. Three letter words (no con. blends) <u>lap</u>
2. Words with final con. blends <u>last</u>
3. Words with initial con. blends <u>slat</u>
4. Words with initial and final con. blends <u>plant</u>

Beginning with letter <u>u</u>, one-syl. words are arranged by length. Initial and final blends are no longer grouped together.

Unless special situation is stated, the letter presented is regular for spelling the sound shown.

Page	Letter Order	Concepts to Develop
4	i(ĭ)	Reading and spelling in initial and medial situation
	t(t)	Blending sounds into words. A vowel in a closed syl. is short. <u>it</u> Marking short vowel with breve. ˘
	p(p)	
	n(n)	Doubled con. are pronounced once. <u>inn</u> Sound pictures omit silent letters. <u>inn</u> (ĭn)
	s̲(s)(z)	s̲ is naturally pronounced (s) after unvoiced con. sounds and (z) after voiced con. sounds. <u>sips</u> <u>sins</u> (z) is regularly spelled s̲ except when initial in a word. <u>is</u> <u>Spelling Rules</u>: The regular plural of a noun is spelled by adding s̲. <u>tips</u>. Third person singular verbs add s̲. <u>He</u> <u>sits</u>.
5	a(ă)	
5	l(l)	
6	d(d)	(d)(t) Voiced and unvoiced partners
7	f(f)	Spelling Rule: One-syl. words ending in (f), (l) or (s) after one vowel usually end in <u>ff</u>, <u>ll</u>, <u>ss</u>. <u>stiff</u>, <u>pill</u>, <u>pass</u>
8	h(h)	
8	g(g)	
9	ng(ng	<u>Suffix Concept</u>: Final <u>ing</u> can be b.w. ending or a suffix. (Is a word left after covering <u>ing</u>? If so, <u>ing</u> is a suffix.) <u>ing</u> can be added to any b.w. ending in two con. with no change to b.w. or suf. (suffix rules for dropping, doubling or changing final letters of b.w. do not apply to these words.)

Page	Letter Order	Concepts to Develop (Cont'd.)
10	o(ŏ)	Recognizing slightly altered sound (ŏ). <u>log</u>
11	m(m)	
11	r(r)	Reading and spelling <u>r</u> when initial in a word or in initial blends. <u>rat</u> <u>trap</u> (Omit <u>r</u>-controlled vowels – er, ir, etc., at this point.) Blending words into sentences.
15	e(ĕ)	Many students will never be able to distinguish between (ĭ) and (ĕ) when it falls before <u>n</u> or <u>m</u>, but they should be aware of the difficulty. <u>Syllable Division</u>: VC´/CV VC/CV´ Beginning with first vowel in a word, write V over vowels and C over consonants. <p style="text-align:center">VCCV fossil</p>Divide between two consonants which stand between two vowels. Determine accent. ar´/rest - - - - - ar/rest´√ den´/tist√- - - - -den/tist´ <u>Syllable Division</u>: VC/CCV VCC/CV with con. blend A consonant blend sticks together in a syl. and behaves as one con. Determine best blend. Divide word. im/press√ imp/ress Determine accent: im´press im press´√ (More often, a single con. will close the first syl.)
19	y(y)	Consonant <u>y</u> is initial in syl. Irregular for spelling except in initial position in word.
	y(ĭ)(ī)	Vowel <u>y</u> takes sounds of <u>i</u>: (ī) at end of accented syl. (1-syl. word is accented.) <u>fly</u> (ĭ) at end of unaccented syl. <u>pen´ny</u> (ĭ) in closed syl. <u>pyg´my</u> <u>Spelling Situation</u>: English words do not end in <u>i</u>. Use <u>y</u>. Read medial <u>y</u>, which behaves as <u>i</u>. Suffix <u>y</u> – (added to base words ending in 2 con.)
21	u(ŭ)	Blending sentences into stories.
26	k(k)	(g) (k) Voiced and unvoiced partners
	nk(ngk)	(ng) (ngk) Voiced and unvoiced partners
27	c(k)(s)	<u>c</u> = (s) before <u>e</u>, <u>i</u> and <u>y</u> <u>c</u> has no sound of its own and appears as (k) or (s) in sound pictures. (ăk´ sĕnt) <u>c</u> (s) is irregular for spelling at this point. <u>Spelling Situation</u>: Initial and Medial (k) 1. Use <u>c</u> unless before <u>e</u>, <u>i</u> and <u>y</u>. 2. Use <u>k</u> before <u>e</u>, <u>i</u>, and <u>y</u>. <u>keg</u> <u>skip</u> <u>sky</u>
31	ck(k)	Digraph = two letters with one sound. Reading <u>ck</u> words. (Spelling final (k) must be delayed until initial and medial situation is thoroughly understood and automatic.)

Page	Letter Order	Concepts to Develop (Cont'd.)
31	ck(k)	Spelling Situation: Final (k) 1. Use ck at end of one-syl. words after short vowel. truck 2. Use k after consonants. sink 3. Use ic to spell (ĭk) at the end of multisyl. words. picnic
33	b(b)	(b) (p) Voiced and unvoiced partners Careful pronunciation: (b), NOT (buh)!
35	j(j)	Final accented vowels are long. A 1-syl. word is accented mē nō Chant: "A vowel at the end of an accented syl. is long." mē "A vowel in a closed syl. is short." mĕt Final o is long regardless of accent. stuc´/co Reading 3-syl. words, dividing between consonants.
39	ed(ĕd) (d) (t)	In multisyl. words, final ed is usually a suffix pronounced (ĕd) (t) (d) Note to TEACHER: ed after d and t = (ĕd); hunted added after unvoiced sound = (t); asked after voiced sound = (d); filled Recognizing and spelling complete base words before adding suffixes. less, ness, ful, ly, en.
40	w(w) wa(wŏ)	
41	v	(v) (f) Voiced and unvoiced partners Eng. words do not end in v but add silent e. give Suffix -ive (ĭv)
42	z(z)	(z) is spelled z only when initial in word.
	x(ks)	Unvoiced
	(gz)	Voiced
46	qu(kw)	qu acts as two cons., k and w. u after a q is not considered a vowel; thus (f) (l) (s) Rule and (k) Spelling Situations apply. quill, quick Spelling Situations: In a 2-syl. word, when only 1 medial con. sound is heard after a short vowel in the first syl., the con. is regularly doubled. rabbit is regular; rob in, irregular. Cons. are not regularly doubled in three-syl. base words. Before proceeding to Level II, the student must recognize con. suffixes less, ness, ful, ly.

i   t   p   n   s

it	nit	pips
is	tip	pins
in	nip	pits
inn	pit	tints
sip	its	sist
sin	it's	spin
sis	sins	snit
tit	nits	spit
tin	sips	snips
sit	tint	spins
pip	inns	stint
pin	nips	stints

****

ip	nint	pisp	spist
iss	sisp	spiss	spints
nin	sint	sniss	spips
niss	ips	stit	stins
tiss	sints	inst	spint
int	ints	spip	stisp
ipt	pinst	stip	snint
nins	tisp	snin	spipt
tist	nist	stin	snisp
nisp	tinst	stiss	stist
inst	nints	snist	spisp

4

a (ă) 🍎

at	nasp	spass	last
as	snap	stans	list
an	spat	stast	lint
ass	span	spant	lilt
Ann	Stan	snast	lisp
pap	stap	stasp	lant
pan		stant	silt
pass	* * * *	spast	Alps
san		snant	tilt
tap	ap	spasp	palp
tan	nass	snans	slit
sap	tant	snasp	plat
sat	nans		slip
sass	pasp	l 🍂	plap
pat	ans		plan
tat	tast	lass	still
nap	nasp	nill	slat
Nan	nant	lap	slap
Nat	sasp	lit	spill
ant	tasp	pal	split
past	snass	ill	splat
sant	spap	lip	plant
pant	snan	till	stilt
asp	stass	Sal	slant
apt	snat	pill	splint
	stat	sill	

5

ilp	spilp	id	pid
lilp	slist	dill	nad
lanst	planst	add	dass
pilp	snilp	did	dat
tilp	plint	dap	dant
nilt	splant	tid	disp
linst	snilt	dip	dilp
plit	splast	pad	dasp
slan	plins	lid	dist
sliss	plist	Dan	dinst
pliss	slasp	diss	dilt
slin	stilp	tad	dast
splass	splinst	Sid	tand
slass	plast	nid	danst
spliss	slisp	dad	snad
plip	splanst	din	spid
splin	slint	sad	plid
splan	splins	diss	snid
snill	plinst	lad	slad
plin	splasp	and	stid
splap	plasp	sand	splad
splip	splist	land	splid
slast	slinst	slid	sland
plilt	slins	spad	spand
slans	plisp	stand	spland

fad	sniff	fant	sliff
fin	flat	ift	plaff
piff	stiff	fint	spaff
fill	flip	filp	fliss
if	spiff	pift	flad
fit	flint	ilf	slaff
fip		fasp	fland
tiff	* * * *	pilf	spaft
fat		naft	slaft
faff	taff	fanst	flant
fan	laff	fift	spilf
fid	fap	filt	plaft
daff	fass	alf	flast
fast	fiff	tilf	slift
lift	naff	dift	flanst
fand	fiss	laft	spift
fist	aff	silf	plift
taft	siff	faft	flasp
aft	paff	finst	snaft
sift	niff	nilf	flins
daft	liff	saft	flist
flap	diff	fliff	flinst
staff	saff	snaff	flift
flan	dilf	flass	splift
flit	nift	flin	splaft
	paft		

h  **g**

had	gag	glid	glan
hill	dig	flag	glaff
has	fag	glad	spig
hiss	fig	gliss	plig
his	gig	glass	slig
hip	gal	snig	glat
hap	dag	slag	flig
hit	gap	snag	glit
hat	hag	gliff	plag
han	nig	stag	glap
hid	gas	gland	glin
Hal	nag	glint	glag
hin	gan		glid
hand	pig	* * * *	stig
hint	gad		glip
hant	sag	ig	splag
hast	lag	pag	splig
hist	gid	lig	glist
haft	gaff	ag	glind
hilt	tig	hig	glast
hasp	tag	gaft	glasp
hasn't	gat	gant	glant
	gilt	gast	glaft
	gasp	hilg	glinst
	gift	gand	glanst
		spag	

sin sing	singing	sifting
pin ping	lifting	hanging
fan fang	tilling	slinging
pan pang	stinging	lisping
din ding	gasping	flinging
tan tang	sanding	ganging
Dan dang	sniffing	dinging
tin ting	hinting	staffing
fling	slanting	tinging
gang	hissing	handing
hang	listing	standing
sting	lilting	landing
slang	spilling	sassing
sling	planting	passing
sang	panting	lasting

==

Dan is gasping – hand is stinging!
Dan at asp his hat is flinging.

9

dot	doss	fod	dog
doll	hot	ot	hog
God	fop	noss	loss
don	Todd	dods	off
got	doff	tont	on
hod	soss	hond	toss
loll	pond	sont	log
gog	golf	nong	oft
hop	opt	hoft	lost
tog	tongs	nosp	soft
lot	fond	polp	song
nod	font	lond	loft
lop	spot	hons	long
fog	stoss	gont	gong
not	flop	sond	gloss
odd	snod	stoff	floss
nog	stop	spod	
pop	slop	ploss	
pot	plod	spoll	
sol	slot	sploss	
top	flog	splot	
sop	plop	stons	
tot	plot	stont	
goff	spong	spond	
pod	ping-pong	plont	

m		r	
am	miss	rag	drip
dim	mitt	rid	strip
ham	moff	rot	strap
lam	imp	raff	trill
him	amps	ram	dross
mog	damp	rig	frog
dam	limp	rill	trod
mad	mist	rod	tram
miff	gimp	rip	grass
mom	gamp	ran	prop
mop	film	rap	from
pam	simp	Ron	priss
mot	mant	rim	grip
mid	tamp	rat	trot
mat	mast	ring	prod
mill	pomp	rang	pram
man	lamp	romp	drill
Tom	Ming	raft	prim
Moll	mang	rant	trim
Sam	slim	rasp	prom
mass	smog	ramp	drop
Tim	smit	dram	grill
moss	slam	drag	grid
map	stomp	trip	Fran
tam	stamp	trap	grim

11

grit
grin
gram
frill
sprig
prong
frond
string
primp
sprang
graft
grift
strong
grant
spring
frost
print
grasp
strand
draft
tromp
gramps
drift
tramp
grand
sprint

L.W.: <u>of</u> <u>the</u> <u>Mr.</u> <u>Mrs.</u> <u>a</u> (ā)

1. Sid is hot. Fran fans him.

2. Stand the flag on the land.

3. Hang the damp rag on the log.

4. Pam nods and grins at Pop.

5. Damp grass has a gloss.

6. The strap on the stand snaps.

7. Pat and tamp and pot the plant.

8. Sit still! The film is grand.

9. I am not fond of figs.

10. The hag dons an odd hat.

11. Print a long list of slang.

12. Fast Dan sprints past the flag.

13. Ann is slim. Dot is fat.

14. Ron is fast at ping-pong.

15. Drill pits and fill the gaps.

16. Mag's dog has lost its tag.

17. As the dog lolls, Mag pats it.

18. Dan has his fist in a splint.

19. I am sad. Dan has his fist in a sling.

20. Miss Moss did miss mass.

21. Fling the string and spin the top.

22. Mom had a flat. Dad had a fit.

23. Grasp the lid and tilt the pan.

24. It is spring. Sniff the plants!

25. Frost is on the glass. It drips.

26. Grip the ring, snap it off, and sip.

27. Tim flips and lands in the drift.

28. Sap drops and Sam slips on it.

29. The stag hid in the drift from the man.

30. The frog hops in the fronds at the pond.

31. The ant sits still on the sill. Splat!

32. An asp stings Sal's hand. Slap it!

33. Is Tom as mad at Pat as Pat is at HIM?

34. If Tom plans a list, Pat stomps off!

35. Rip hops and plops and flips and flops.

36. Drop, plip, plop. The tap drips.

37. The rag doll naps in the tot's lap.

38. Don fills a glass and spills his pop.

39. The glass gong rings as it is hit.

40. Pal rang it and ran, and sat and hid!

41. Mr. and Mrs. Pitts pass in the smog on the hill.

42. The rim of the pot is hot. The pan's rim is not.

43. Sid got a flat-top. I got a trim.

44. In a tiff, Tag got a fat, stiff lip.

45. A rat slips past Al. Al is glad!

46. I am strong as I sing. The song lasts long!

47. Dad tills the sod and plants the pods.

48. The tramp was hit in the hip and limps.

49. Hal tamps his hand print in the sand.

50. Tom trips on a damp ramp. Nan mops it.

51. Lon lists on his stilts and drops off.

(ĭ)   (ĕ)

dell	–	dill		pip	–	pep
fell		fill		reg		rig
hill		hell				
let		lit		tin		ten
led		lid		pin		pen
lift		left		din		den
mess		miss		fen		fin
mitt		met		him		hem
net		nit		men		Min
pig		peg		tint		tent
rid		red				
sill		sell		* * * * * * * *		
rit		ret				
set		sit		hiff	–	heff
fet		fit		mip		mep
tell		till		seff		siff
pit		pet		heg		hig
ill		ell		tilp		telp
meg		mig		dist		dest
fest		fist		driff		dreff
mill		mell		gress		griss
press		priss		pred		prid
sneg		snig		dret		drit
slid		sled		sprip		sprep
spell		spill		treff		triff
				sprill		sprell

egg	mend	rent	dentist
leg	help	nest	errand
fed	eft	fret	gospel
hen	fend	sled	herring
Ned	deft	Greg	infant
Nell	pent	Fred	lesson
Meg	helm	dress	magnet
get	heft	glen	mitten
met	lens	press	pallet
sen	held	fled	pregnant
el	dent	step	seldom
em	melt	stet	happen
fet	pest	sned	trellis
Ted	lend	stem	goddess
mell	pelt	sped	helmet
less	rest	spled	
hep	rend	smell	VC/CV´
pep	sent	tress	
sell	test	stress	intend
fess	tend	spent	indent
ebb	self	slept	pastel
elf	lent	spend	enlist
elm	send	smelt	arrest
end	hemp	trend	attend
felt	lest	prest	offend
			attempt

16

VC´/CV, VC/CV´

aspen	random	horrid	limpet
allot	ramrod	tassel	mammon
admit	sonnet	impend	mental
impel	sorrel	intent	Mongol
ingot	tomtom	mammal	linnet
onset	signal	mantis	pennon
Islam	tinsel	infest	pepsin
gallop	terret	maggot	lintel
gossip	signet	inning	lippet
fossil	torrid	linden	pampas
annals	fennel	madras	Nimrod
ferret	pellet	limbus	damsel
addend	tennis	parrot	sodden
assist	tiptop	pistil	lignin
dental	tonsil	pistol	missal
damson	festal	pompon	Dallas
garret	fillip	insist	Lipton
gallon	tandem	limpid	tetrad
mallet	tendon	telson	dolman
assent	gammon	mantel	lepton
attest	append	millet	raglan
dismal	errant	Nippon	dollop
dispel	assess	poplin	heptad
ransom	hostel	piston	Dennis
sandal	hamlet	pallid	ransom

pigment	figment	entrap	ripplet
gallant	pontiff	astral	nonstop
gosling	midriff	offset	distress
dismiss	pennant	instep	eggplant
distant	regnant	Alfred	transmit
segment	trodden	inspan	flimflam
trammel	distend	empress	mistress
plastid	Preston	address	mattress
transit	tempest	gingham	misprint
rampant	lemming	impress	ramstram
flannel	linsang	instill	misspell
transom	trippet	mongrel	riffraff
possess	smitten	nostril	slipslop
stopgap	horrent	implant	handsel
Finland	torrent	misstep	plastron
flotsam	distill	imprint	Tristram
gremlin	Stetson	instant	spindrift
griffin	Dresden	oppress	spindling
grapnel	flippant	ringlet	standstill
Trenton	fragment	ingress	transplant
hapless	stagnant	entrant	transgress
grommet	splendid	pilgrim	helmsman
mastiff	stedfast	tendril	hamstring
pendant	trespass	gastrin	handgrip
pendent	transept	tangram	handspring

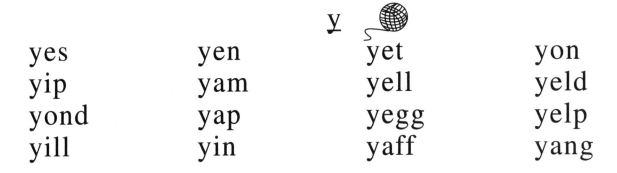

y

yes	yen	yet	yon
yip	yam	yell	yeld
yond	yap	yegg	yelp
yill	yin	yaff	yang

Vowel y

When does vowel y = (ī)? (ĭ)?

Remember that a one-syllable word is accented.

(ī)	(ĭ)	(ī)	(ĭ)
fly	pen´ny	ap ply´	dan´dy
dry	hap´py	im ply´	gran´ny
fry	dad´dy	al ly´	nas´ty
my	mer´ry	es py´	hol´ly
ply	sil´ly		
pry	plen´ty		
sly	emp´ty		
spy	fif´ty		
try	han´dy		

Pronounce these words carefully with the final (ĭ) sound. This will be a spelling help.

Sally	pansy	pantry	trolly
Molly	petty	daffy	nifty
Patsy	angry	ditty	natty
Harry	dolly	ferry	dilly
marry	mammy	sissy	flimsy

19

Vowel y

filly	toddy	eddy	pappy
tipsy	sloppy	tarry	lolly
lorry	tansy	gantry	poppy
folly	dally	giddy	middy
soggy	testy	soppy	grisly
sorry	Denny	haply	nanny
nappy	Emmy	harry	Kerry
slimsy	Henry	sonsy	Larry
patty	sentry	rally	tally
taffy	parry	ninny	entry

Suffix y

sandy	stringy	pesty	dressy
frilly	prissy	sassy	tangy
glassy	filmy	hilly	frosty
drafty	messy	grassy	smelly

Medial y

Lynn	pygmy	hymnal
rynt	symptom	allyl
Flynn	mistryst	hyssop
tymp	hymnist	tympan
Fyn	system	fylfot

u (ŭ)

up	gust	lull	fluff
us	dust	smug	flung
fud	gull	runt	snuff
rug	glum	hull	grunt
gup	lump	dunt	truss
mug	smut	spug	dunst
tug	pulp	muss	drunt
hug	dult	tuft	stuff
rum	rust	puff	stung
rut	ruff	must	mumps
sum	plug	sung	drung
hut	mull	glut	slump
gun	pump	muff	flump
gum	spun	dump	plump
pug	huff	plum	strut
mum	drug	stud	spung
sup	suds	snug	slung
hum	lung	fuss	trump
fun	drum	spud	strum
gut	fuff	rung	stunt
pun	punt	rump	gruff
nun	slum	stun	stump
ump	dull	hung	trust
gulf	fund	slug	strung
tump	gulp	hump	sprung

u (ŭ)   VCCV, VCCCV

funny	possum	sundry	plummet
gully	unless	larrup	grampus
mummy	hungry	summon	humdrum
fuffy	tunnel	puffin	gunnung
until	puppet	mullet	frustum
gunny	fustet	palpus	fruggan
puppy	gullet	tittup	grummel
upset	sullen	leptus	tantrum
guffy	insult	supply	lustrum
annul	gulden	rumpus	sistrum
ruddy	sultry	sudden	entrust
fusty	summit	Talmud	disrupt
muggy	mussel	muslin	stuffing
lusty	mutton	Muslem	mistrust
dummy	fungus	unrest	doldrums
tunny	Dustin	magnum	suppress
hussy	russet	fundus	huntress
sully	muffin	hundred	dandruff
mufti	funnel	suspend	supplant
guppy	nugget	trumpet	tungsten
tummy	sultan	mustang	lustring
yummy	engulf	disgust	stunning
ugly	gusset	glutton	flustrum
grundy	nutmeg	nostrum	distrust
guffin	fungal	yum-yum	hamstrung

Review

* *

nad	nass	dran	flut
het	feg	telp	drump
pid	niff	drist	tesp
fot	foss	flod	prang
sug	lup	funt	stylf
nyg	naff	glest	gling
pag	sep	demp	grud
med	fiss	prit	prosp
mip	goll	flot	plast
hom	fut	gusp	stolp
nud	fyp	prag	flunt
ryll	fap	drell	ang
dass	leff	fing	frid
det	fim	dosp	stren
hig	hon	flust	frug
foll	duss	felp	grig
fug	rass	preff	somp
syn	tep	spid	smed
fass	neg	droll	glud
fem	dyt	flum	strim
niss	tet	smad	trond
fod	heg	fless	smat
ung	lig	dilt	reld
myp	oss	drod	flunst
fam	fum	dulp	splung

The Merry Mutt

Pug Ugly is a daffy dog, a merry mutt! He has fun as he digs in the dump! From sun-up to sunset, Pug has dug up:

a signet ring,
a pellet gun,
a flannel rug,
a tuft of mattress,
a snip of red muslin,
a lass's fluffy muff,
a fragment of a fossil, and
a pennant from P.U.! Pug huffs and puffs as he sniffs and tugs at the musty, dusty stuff. He sets it in a gallon of H_2O from the pump, and adds suds. The stuff is hung up to dry. The pellet gun and signet ring possess rust. The rust is gotten off.

Pug can pry into the tin hut at the end of the dump. It's sloppy and smelly and drafty. "If it's MY hut, I must prop it on struts so it is less flimsy. And it's DULL –

24

dismal and dull! If it's MY hut, I must get grass and pansy and poppy plants. I'll set the hut's mess into a hump and lug in MY stuff. I'll fling the flannel rug. I'll pin up the red muslin. I'll hang up tinsel and tassels and pompons!"

The daffy dog runs and hums. The nutty mongrel flits and struts. He is so fond of his Pug Ugly Hut, the merry mutt plans to tend the dump by himself.

He adds a segment to his felt pennant and hangs it on the entry.

Yes?/No?

Is a gremlin an elf? Is a yam a spud?
Do magnets help eggplant to fry?
Has tinsel a gloss? Is a yo-yo a pup?
Do possums do handsprings and fly?

k

king	sink	tusk	trinket
sky	honk	frisk	husky
kid	ink	slink	musket
keg	kink	hulk	kremlin
kin	plank	drink	inkling
kiln	trunk	drank	pumpkin
skit	plunk	drunk	Kipling
kill	yank	skulk	gasket
kiss	punk	flank	plisky
skin	pink	plink	numskull
ken	link	skunk	skinflint
kelp	rank	skink	kestrel
kemp	**k, nk**	husk	griskin
kef	hunk	stink	sulky
kist	ask	stank	kelpy
kilt	dusk	rink	plankton
skill	sank	task	Franklin
kit	elk	dank	napkin
skimp	hank	tank	skinking
klong	disk		mollusk
skim	flunk	Kellogg	hunky
yak	risk	anklet	kennel
skiff	sulk	flunky	skillet
kip	spunk	kismet	kindred
skull	musk	honky-tonk	muskrat

c (k)

cup	clam	cliff	hiccup
cap	crag	scrag	traffic
cot	clot	crust	crystal
cam	cram	scamp	contest
cud	camp	can't	comment
cry	clog	scrod	canyon
cod	clan	crimp	cactus
cog	scop	scalp	command
cat	clip	canst	confess
con	culm	cling	consist
cop	scup	crypt	cotton
cut	cusp	scrim	crimson
cuff	clump	cramp	carrot
scan	clink	clung	casket
cask	scrap	crest	commit
clap	class	clamp	common
cast	crisp	Scott	caftan
scum	scuff	scrat	consent
cult	cross	scull	discuss
scat	scoff	scrip	discus
scud	crept	scram	hectic
clod	clang	sclaff	mystic
clop	clank	scrimp	consult
crop	clasp	script	constant
cull	crank	scruff	campus

catnip	cranny	spastic
clumsy	rascal	scalpel
collop	cutlet	styptic
metric	congress	dictum
fiscal	custom	cosmos
canny	frantic	scrannel
tocsin	sanctum	cryptic
picnic	septic	falcon
rustic	plastic	lactic
mastic	carry	sculpin
consul	tactics	transcript
acrid	contrast	spectrum
caddis	codling	conscript
coffin	culprit	hepcat
caddy	Lettic	compress
ascot	optic	scandal
compel	canton	skeptic
commend	occult	encrust
cutlass	contempt	crisscross
ferric	classic	spectral
muscat	clammy	tannic
mascot	peptic	Scranton
contend	crafty	handcuff
cosmic	accost	Scotland
aspic	content	descant

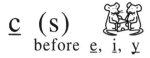
act	suspect	Cid	cystid
duct	afflict	cit	citric
tract	contact	cyst	citron
fact	prospect	cess	ascent
tact	conflict	cell	cygnet
Pict	distinct	cent	citrin
pact	district	celt	cestus
mulct	distract	cest	Cedric
strict	attract	cist	princess
addict	conduct	scend	crescent
affect	pandect	scent	central
effect	inspect	cinct	stencil
intact	contract		cinclis
concoct	compact	fancy	suscept
neglect	inflict	Nancy	scissel
impact	instinct	cancel	concept
insect	transect	citrus	centrum
aspect	instruct	pencil	
collect	constrict	ascend	accent
dissect	connect	rancid	accept
induct	inflect	dulcet	access
infect	construct	census	success
		incept	flaccid
		lancet	succinct

29

<u>c</u> (k)   (s)

* *

caff	cund	<u>sc</u>	
ceff	cim	scep	criff
ciff	clid	scun	sciff
cung	cyll	scim	scag
cym	cren	scod	clyn
cep	cilt	scell	cin
com	clyd	scass	scyll
clyt	cosp	scrad	ciss
cyg	cyd	scyd	crypt
crip	cang	scip	scyn
ceg	creff	scon	colp
cun	cisp	scen	casp
comp	cas	scang	cyss
cred	clym	scill	scest
clep	crill	scoss	scit
cint	celp	scuss	cuft
ced	cust	sciss	cimp

When is final (k) spelled <u>ck</u>? <u>k</u>? <u>c</u>?

sick	elk	picnic
sack	sank	attic
luck	tusk	frantic
peck	silk	traffic
clock	mollusk	mystic

			A few multi-syllable words end <u>ck</u>:
truck	stick	crock	
track	stock	crick	
duck	tick	hick	haddock
Dick	tack	hock	attack
deck	tuck	hack	derrick
dock	tock	huck	paddock
lock	clack	flick	ransack
lack	cluck	nick	mattock
lick	click	neck	hammock
sock	pluck	smock	cassock
pack	rack	smack	hemlock
stuck	rock	prick	hassock
pick	rick	speck	hillock
pock	muck	cock	hummock
puck	Mack	struck	lipstick
stack	mock	kick	traprock
fleck	plick	crack	gimmick
suck	plack	sneck	fetlock

1. Pat is tops at passing.
   Tad is tops at kicking.

2. Hal is acting in a film.
   Sal is singing in its cast.

3. Sis's milk is spilling.
   Crack! Clinking glass!

4. Mack is getting sick, and Mom
   is handing him a hot drink.

5. Mag is tinting a smock pink.
   It is not costing a lot.

6. Tom is stacking pants.
   Tim is packing slacks.

7. Is the clock standing flat?
   Its ticking stops if it tilts.

8. Dad is asking Nan facts.
   Jan is adding 7+7 and 8+8.

9. Tim is panting from his sprint.
   Kim is gasping in Tim's fast tracks.

10. Is Sam missing a sock?
    No, Sam is socking a miss!

b

bat	fib	belt	stub
bag	cub	drub	band
bug	bib	slub	brod
big	bus	bunt	block
bog	hub	brad	black
beg	sob	bass	bland
bet	tub	blab	blink
bit	glib	bend	brick
but	buff	bust	bliss
bed	bask	blat	blimp
bud	best	bond	brass
bid	crab	brog	blunt
bad	bulb	bulk	blast
rib	crib	brit	blank
rub	bilk	gamb	brand
rob	grab	buck	blend
dub	bing	back	bluff
Ben	bump	brab	brack
nab	blob	bund	bract
gab	brag	bank	blond
gob	club	brig	brisk
dab	blot	bank	bless
bun	bell	bent	scrub
cob	bran	bung	brink
cab	bled	brim	brunt

b

absent	ballad	tymbal
tablet	bantam	cymbal
public	abstract	rabbit
hobby	abscess	hobnob
bonnet	ballast	bandy
blanket	symbol	emboss
bandit	submit	bedlam
basket	stubby	gambrel
berry	obstruct	hubbub
tabby	problem	niblick
subtract	bannock	umbrel
husband	billet	subsist
buggy	dobbin	goblet
fabric	gambit	bombast
button	barren	lambent
belly	bonny	timbrel
barrel	humbug	baptism
album	lobby	Dublin
ballot	brandy	Lisbon
Baptist	abscond	nimbus
bottom	barracks	tumbrel
combat	batting	bodkin
oblong	sibling	bonbon
bunny	emblem	bumpkin
bobbin	Brussels	buttress

jam	adjust	banjo	canto
just	jelly	ditto	limbo
jig	subject	hello	mango
junk	jiffy	motto	dingo
Jeff	Jimmy	stucco	rondo
jut	inject	tango	lingo
jack	jolly	lasso	umbo
jab	junket	fresco	Oslo
Jill	jenny	grotto	junto
jag	jetsam	hippo	jingo
jib	jennet	gumbo	bingo
Jap	jetty	jello	crambo
jumb	object	presto	Anglo
joss	adjunct	tempo	gringo
jest	jessant	gusto	pinto
jug	jundy	alto	junco
jot	jetton	lotto	Ringo
jink	jutty	jumbo	ningpo
jet	Jerry	Crisco	combo
jog	Jenkins	campo	gingko
jilt	Justin	Enco	Sambo
job	juggins	Otto	hullo
jad	muntjac	cisco	cento
Jan	jim-jams	banco	fungo
Jess		Mumbo	Jumbo

35

Atlantic	concensus	bilberry
badminton	insistent	cantonment
amnesty	accustom	prognostic
assembly	embankment	inconstant
confetti	embassy	intrinsic
cranberry	indignant	loblolly
embarrass	musketry	encampment
fantastic	intellect	Carrollton
assassin	symmetry	albescent
tendency	incessant	disconnect
industry	gallantry	Alcestis
infantry	concentric	eclectic
hobgoblin	ballistics	Gillingham
dentistry	bankruptcy	incumbent
dickcissal	commitment	dyspeptic
Manhattan	attendant	indistinct
hagberry	bombastic	commandment
asbestos	sacristy	malcontent
constancy	lemniscus	palmetto
eccentric	Hottentot	alfresco
infancy	husbandry	fandango
adjustment	encompass	castellan
ancestry	agnostic	contralto
assistant	backgammon	Connally
mulberry	ascendant	systaltic

Princess Priss

Priscíllot, the Princess of Loddom-y-Dot,

(In the District of Dulcet, in Land of the Lot)

Sniffs, "I got the HICCUPS! Disgusting! I'll let

Six Mystics assist me. I just must not fret!"

___

△I "Priscíllot, track cygnets on Princess Pond!"

△II "Collect red insects from off a frond!

△III "Go fly a falcon kept in a hut!"

△IV "Inspect the kennels and pat a mutt!"

△V "Conduct a census of ants in the sand!"

△VI "Cancel a fifty-cent stamp of Lot Land!"

△I "Go loll in a hammock strung onto a banyon!"

△II "Ascend yon hill. Descend into canyon!"

△III "Concoct fancy muffins – the scent is fantastic!"

△IV "Try testing effects of wax pencils on plastic!"

△V "Construct a cell hidden by moss and by rocks!"

△VI "Go romp by the ducks and the hens and the cocks!"

Priscíllot, the Princess of Loddom-y-Dot,

(In the District of Dulcet, in Land of the Lot)

Puffs, "I TRY Mystic plans. Still the hic-cups distress.

But long sniffs in a citrus-scent sack get success!"

===

9:00 P.M.

O, I <u>rib</u> <u>reb</u> rub in the <u>tib</u> <u>teb</u> tub
As I <u>scrib</u> <u>screb</u> scrub upon my back!
I sip <u>Tub</u> <u>Tob</u> Tab, just a <u>dub</u> <u>dob</u> dab,
As I <u>gub</u> <u>gob</u> gab and "hit the sack!"

Suffix <u>ed</u>

(t)	(d)	(ed)
kicked	smelled	tested
passed	filmed	tilted
puffed	banged	drifted
asked	egged	ended
helped	happened	added

missed	jelled	printed	honked
filled	bumped	skilled	mended
acted	lasted	limped	hanged
fussed	packed	camped	flocked
hunted	yelled	hinted	lulled
fluffed	dusted	dulled	tinted
melted	lifted	slanted	ganged
spelled	dumped	risked	gulped
huffed	rusted	culled	granted
killed	spilled	blinked	bonged
kissed	bucked	clanged	lucked
dented	sifted	nested	drafted
blocked	hulled	planted	blasted
panted	punted	cranked	stilled
drilled	cocked	milled	clamped
banked	flunked	flocked	ebbed
longed	tended	mulled	yanked

<u>w</u>

web	wept	willet	<u>wa</u> (wŏ)
wig	swig	wigwag	swat
win	wist	widdy	wasp
wit	wend	welkin	swap
wet	weft	wintry	wand
wed	welk	wonky	swab
wem	swell	wombat	want
well	swift	Widbin	swan
wink	Swiss	witness	watt
wilt	swing	wedlock	wan
twin	dwell	wistful	´twas
west	twang	Winston	swamp
wisp	twill	winglet	wap
swam	swank	Wilhelm	was
wick	twist	winnock	wad
swum	twink	witling	wampum
weld	swept	wigging	wanton
wing	swill	windmill	wigwam
twig	dwang	gromwell	wallop
wind		windswept	wampus
welt	Willis	Wisconsin	warrant
twit	wisdom	wittingly	Watson
will	twenty	Wilmington	wallet
went	Wilson	Wellington	Wankel
swim	Weldon	willy-nilly	walrus

40

v

van
vim
vet
vat
vast
vest
vamp
vent
vang
Vick

envy
Elvis
salvo
velvet
vandal
invest
canvas
victim
vessel
pelvis
invent
advent
viscid
sylvan

vulcan
vespid
vassal
viscus
vestry
convict
convent
ventral
solvent
vestment
victress
solvency

English words do not end in v. Silent e is added.

have
lĭve
give
solve
valve
salve
delve
twelve
involve
dissolve

ive (ĭv) may be a final syllable of a baseword or it may be a suffix.

pensive
jussive
adjective
incentive
invective
submissive
vindictive
attentive

What is the baseword?

active
massive
inductive
inventive
attractive
collective
corrective
effective
objective
possessive
successive
constructive
instinctive

41

z   <u>x</u> (ks)

oz	ziffs	box	sex
sip	frizz	ox	pyx
fez		ax	zax
Liz	dizzy	mix	nix
zig	zombi	wax	text
zed	Aztec	six	next
Zen	fuzzy	tax	flex
zag	tizzy	fix	flax
tez	Uzbek	fox	lynx
Zan	zambo	lax	crux
zep	Zanni	Tex	Styx
zac	zorro	lux	flux
Boz	zemmi	pax	stryx
adz	zimbi	sox	
buzz	donzel	sax	annex
jazz	benzyl	Nyx	index
zest	mizzen	kex	affix
fuzz	frenzy	rux	excel
zinc	Zambis	Nox	expel
razz	zemmis	pox	sixty
zing	zigzag	vex	infix
fizz	grizzly	Rex	oxlip
Zend	pretzel	Max	addax
zizz	zingsang	hex	convex
Zack	Zamzummen	tux	suffix

excess
syntax
expand
Windex
Lennox
sexton
except
extent
expend
sextet
expect
extant
Wessex
paxwax
exsect
Mannix
extend
hallux
influx
pinxit
Caxton
complex
flummox
extinct
extract

detrin
express
context
Maxwell
exscind
Hystrix
transfix
appendix
expresso
sixpenny
excellent
extrinsic
extensive

x may divide (k/s)

k/s

Texas (těk´săs)
taxi
axis
axil
maxim
doxy
pixy
hexad
Nixon
Saxon

pyxis
hexyl
plexus
braxy
toxin
axom
maxi
lixive
caxon
nyxis
toxic
proxy
vixen
taxus
taxis
Lexington
vexillum

x may divide (g/z)

g/z

exist (ěg zǐst´)
exempt
exult
exact
exam
exit

Punt, Pass and Kick

Ted wanted to be the best in the class in punting and constantly tested himself. He slanted the and punted it. It listed to the left and drifted into the long grass. He hunted it, planted it on a dot, tilted it, and tended it intently. At last it swept up and up and up. He added up – six attempts. His "If I try, if I try –" got him success.

Pat kicked and blocked well, but he got hacked off in passing. He clicked off toss #1, but it passed past his pal's hands. He banked on toss #2 to go well, but conked his pal! He packed a wallop into pass #3, but it missed getting to his buddy. He risked try #4, but bucked try #5. He felt he had flunked and limped off.

Rod longed to be the best of the lot at kicking. He planned on his pals' help, and Hal filmed his attempts. He spilled #1 into the pond, and banged into Hal on try #2. A skilled kick winged cross the sticks at last, but it was try #12! He had egged himeslf on and mulled, "I bet I can, I bet I can . . ." and he did! He bonged his helmet on the grass and grinned.

In multisyllable words final _ed_ is nearly always a suffix.

(t)	(d)	(ed)
gossiped	happened	invented
attacked	signaled	insisted
galloped	ransomed	attended
expressed	funneled	collected
impressed	summoned	disgusted
discussed	instilled	contented
ransacked	compelled	suspended
distressed	mispelled	consulted
handcuffed	accustomed	commanded
embarrassed	backgammoned	subtracted

I'm mended and smelled-up, and dressed to
      a "T" - - -
A stuffy class pic! (I'm mad as can be!)

My dog's wonky, honky-tonky,
My dog wags and gets so vexed.
My dog's flappy, happy, scrappy.
My dog's yappy. NANCY's next!

qu (kw) 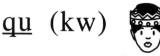   ## qua (kwŏ)   22-24

squint	conquest	qua	* * * *
quell	acquit	quab	guess
quiz	banquet	quan	squit
squid	jonquil	quad	*squam
quip	inquest	squad	quimp
quilt	tranquil	squat	*quass
quest	quinsy	squab	squest
squib	quisby	quarrel	*quall
quit	quintan	quadrant	queck
quint	questing	quarry	squig
quid	quidnunc	quantum	queff
quo	quicksand	quassin	*quand
quin	quintet	quasky	quing
squiss	quitrent	quannet	quem
quap	quondam	quandong	squeg
quod	Squaxon	squadron	
qued	squinny		*Two possible
quiff	quiddit	Why double l?	pronunciations.
squill	quillet	Double f?	
quink	quantic	Why ck?	
quet	squacco	quill	
quib	quincunx	quaff	
quant	quilling	quick	
quag	Algonquin	quack	
quill	quintetto		

Base Word + Two Suffixes

helpfully
helplessness
helplessly
helpfulness
restlessness
restfully
restlessly
restfulness
tactlessness
tactlessly
tactfully
willingly
willingness
willfully
willfulness

fretfully
fretfulness
endlessness
endlessly
fecklessness
fecklessly
zestfully
zestlessly
fittingly
fitfully
skillfully
trustingly
sinfully
slantingly
blissfully

Recognize Final ive + Suffix ly or ness

objectively
excessively
expensively
impulsively
collectively
correctively
attractively
instinctively

massiveness
effectiveness
inventiveness
impassiveness
impressiveness
possessiveness
distinctiveness
constructiveness

Pronounce the Nonsense Words:

1. litten
2. padfom
3. dasrog
4. slignit
5. mangpod
6. mistan
7. spodlit
8. homref
9. gradnol
10. omtod
11. asgot
12. kirry
13. espem
14. plastig
15. smitress
16. prodlet
17. neplas
18. esgot
19. sollast
20. glesning
21. pridgom
22. lassit
23. holpin
24. sprigness
25. egron
26. glamton
27. spliggot
28. sprannet
29. pollom
30. grabbel
31. hedret
32. orry
33. trostil
34. glapnif
35. yesbit
36. brenny
37. gridlet
38. quiglent
39. revbin
40. yerry
41. wannell
42. quattent
43. vestig
44. quisset
45. tresben
46. wevtil
47. zebbet
48. jupnel
49. yasget
50. wamlin
51. blutton

The Picnic

The hungry lads plan a picnic. Jack gets his back pack on. In it he fits a sack, a snack, and an insect can. Tom straps on HIS back pack. In it he fits a sack, long sticks, and a tin cup.

Jack and Tom do not go fast. The sun is hot and the trip is long. Trod and plod. Plod and trod. Tom tramps well, but Jack pants and lags.

Picnic fun? Jack hops on a leg at the rim of the pond and flicks pollen from buds. He rips a web strung on a twig, and pats his hand print into the mud. Tom flits cross slick grass and skips rocks on the pond. He rubs the soft moss on a trunk, and jabs at an ant hill.

The ants attack and sting! Tricky Jack grabs his can of BUG OFF. Press, p-s-s-t! Press, p-s-s-t! And no ants on Tom!

At last the lads stop at a spot by the pond. Tom gets sticks into a stack. Jack fits his and Tom's hotdogs onto the long sticks. The hotdogs get red hot on the grill, drip, and split.

Jack sits on a log, snaps the top off a can of pink pop and sips it. Tom sits by the log and drinks milk from his tin cup. Grilled hotdogs on buns, wet drinks, and a Snack Pack. M-m-m-m-m! Tom and Jack smack lips!

Sand is kicked on the still-hot stack of sticks. The grilling sticks get tossed into the pond. Scraps and cans go into plastic bags in the back packs.

Glad lads sing a song on the long trip back at sunset.

♫ Hi ho, hi ho,
On picnics we can go.
No clocks, no gal,
Just snacks and pal,   ♫
Hi ho, hi ho!

The Spelling Class

quickly	sadness	exactly
badly	restful	splendidly
wanly	sinful	suddenly
limply	randomly	distinctly
fondly	expressly	commonly
aptly	strictly	listlessness
oddly	rampantly	indignantly
lastly	helpless	contentedly
dotless	cunningly	consistently
illness	wistfully	incorrectness
dismally	constantly	unexpectedly

Miss Pell: The clock has said it's spelling, class.

Get crafty and cunning, lads and lass!

We Spell S.O.S

From my randomly-picked list I want Stan to spell <u>sent</u>, as "I <u>sent</u> Mom a gift." <u>Sent</u>.

Stan: <u>Sent</u>. <u>S-e-n-t</u>. And the <u>cent</u> as in "It cost a <u>cent</u>" is <u>c-e-n-t</u>.

Webb: And <u>scent</u> as in "It had a <u>scent</u>" is <u>s-c-e-n-t</u>!

Miss Pell: Yes! Stan and Webb spell and sell and smell well! Rod is next!

Bick: Rod? Insects attacked him rampantly on the hands. Rod slapped them indignantly, but the wasps stung him swiftly. It was grim! The swelling was bad, Rod felt helpless, and his mom sped him off. The doc had to inject him quickly and said Rod must spend a restful bit in bed!

Miss P: Yes? Expressly as his best pal, Bick, spell sadness.

Bick: Sadness. S-a-d-n-e-s-s.

Miss P: As Rod's stand-in, Bick did well! Rod can rest contentedly! Tim, spell misspell.

Tim: M-m-m-m-m?

Miss P: Kim, spell misspell.

Kim: M-m-m-m-m?

Miss P: Spring has affected the twins and listlessness has set in! Tim and Kim wistfully want to get off from class, yes?

Tim and Kim: M-m-m hum-m-m!

Miss P: Jack, spell misspell.

Jack: Misspell. M-i-s-s-p-e-l-l.

Miss P: It was spelled unexpectedly well! Misspell is constantly misspelled! Is Cal back?

Ted: Not yet! I felt badly as the bat I slung hit him in the neck! It sent him off wanly and limply. Cal and I got non-hitting stints from the boss man!

Miss P: Ted, do Cal's spelling. Spell sorry.

Ted: Sorry. S-o-r-r-y. And am I sorry! It is dismally dull if Cal is not in class!

Miss P: Yes. Rod and Cal add a lot. Ben, spell expressed.

Ben: <u>Expressed</u>. <u>E</u>-<u>x</u>-<u>p</u>-<u>r</u>-<u>e</u>-<u>s</u>-<u>s</u>-<u>e</u>-<u>d</u>.

Miss P: Splendidly expressed! The last (t) is the suffix <u>ed</u>, isn't it?

Mel got bitten suddenly by a bug, but his illness did not last past dusk. Fast-getting-well Mel, spell <u>strictly</u>.

Mel: <u>Strictly</u>. <u>S</u>-<u>t</u>-<u>r</u>-<u>i</u>-<u>c</u>-<u>t</u>-<u>l</u>-<u>y</u>.

Miss P: Yes! Strictly in fun, Dot, spell <u>dot-less</u>.

Dot: <u>Dotless</u>. <u>D</u>-<u>o</u>-<u>t</u>-<u>l</u>-<u>e</u>-<u>s</u>-<u>s</u>.

Miss P: Correct! Jud, spell <u>sinful</u>.

Jud: <u>Sinful</u>. <u>S</u>-<u>i</u>-<u>n</u>-<u>f</u>-<u>u</u>-<u>l</u>-<u>l</u>.

Miss P: No, it was spelled oddly at the end. The suffix <u>ful</u> is commonly spelled - - - - -.

Jud: Yes, yes, yes! <u>Sinful</u>. <u>S</u>-<u>i</u>-<u>n</u>-<u>f</u>-<u>u</u>-<u>l</u>.

Miss P: Yes! Lastly, let us spell - - - - - -.

It is sinful to spell <u>sinful</u> sinfull.

54

CLANG! CLANG!

Dot: The bell consistently disrupts us!

Miss P: Aptly said, Dot.

> The random list was cunningly spelled.
> My respect, my gallants, is fondly
>   held!

Class dismissed!

My Pet Rabbit

Algonquin in the back grass,
As tranquil as can be,
Banqueted on jonquil bulbs
And sulked expectantly.
> Squatting by the blossoms
> Was a tom, a fitful cat.
> He quizzed himself, "Must I attack?"
> He squinted, "Yes, a spat!"
>> Algonquin had a quarrel,
>> Algonquin had a tiff.
>> The tomcat had a conquest –
>> Algonquin limped back stiff!

SPOT THE ODD

Read each line and decide which word is unlike the others in meaning.

1. bandit   vandal   culprit   <u>victim</u>

2. tenpins   racket   magnet   discus

3. Scotland   Preston   Holland   Finland

4. skipping   hopping   spitting   jumping

5. punt   kick   pass   class

6. Sally   Larry   Molly   Patsy

7. Dallas   Texas   Kansas   Kentucky

8. Alfred   Pam   Kenneth   Henry

9. golfing   swelling   tennis   swimming

10. mantis   wasp   elk   ant

11. silk   pistol   muslin   flannel

12. trumpet   cymbal   strum   drum

13. skidded   sky   slipped   slid

14. tonsils   pencils   lungs   tendons

SPOT THE ODD

Read each line and decide which word is unlike the others in meaning.

1. truck   <u>puck</u>   van   pick-up
2. sling   fling   floss   toss
3. hands   lungs   mittens   lips
4. dog   cat   pond   pig
5. desk   rust   rug   lamp
6. swan   duck   parrot   swamp
7. slacks   pans   pants   socks
8. sack   basket   back   bag
9. skin   hip   barrel   rib
10. disk   inn   hut   tent
11. land   sand   sod   lob
12. brass   bass   herring   cod
13. eggs   legs   carrots   milk
14. lump   trump   hump   bump

C **B** **A** **K**

Preparation: Complete understanding of open and closed syl., causing long or short vowel: <u>he</u>   <u>hep</u>

Recognition of con. suf. <u>less</u>, <u>ness</u>, <u>ful</u>, <u>ly</u>, <u>s</u>

Letter Order	Concepts to Develop

a-e*   (ā)

a-e   (ē)

i-e   (ī)

o-e   (ō)

u-e   (ū)

(o͞o)

y-e   (ī)

<u>In Reading:</u>

Final <u>e</u> is usually silent

Final <u>e</u> after <u>one</u> con. causes preceding vowel to be long.
   <u>prīce</u>   <u>prĭnce</u>

<u>r</u> may slightly alter a preceding long vowel sound.
   <u>bāre</u>**

<u>u</u>-<u>e</u> = (o͞o) after <u>l</u>, <u>r</u>, or <u>s</u>, since (ū) is difficult to pronounce in these positions.   <u>Luke</u>   <u>rule</u>   <u>capsule</u>

Note: The syl. <u>ture</u> is pronounced (cho͝or) and is explained on p. 246.

Recognizing V-e base word plus con. suffixes <u>less</u>, <u>ness</u>, <u>ful</u>, <u>ly</u>, <u>s</u>. <u>hopeless</u> is not pronounced (hō´pē lĕss). (Important!)

<u>In Spelling:</u>
V-<u>e</u> is reg. spelling of long vowels in final closed syl.

<u>y</u>-<u>e</u> irregular for spelling.

<u>Spelling Situation:</u>
final (k) after long vowel = <u>ke</u>, <u>cake</u>.

Con. suf. does not change spelling of any b.w.
   (EXCEPT if b.w. ends in <u>y</u> – to be studied later).

After the V-<u>e</u> concept is well-learned, these important common exceptions can be learned with sound pictures to show their irregularity: <u>come</u>, <u>some</u>, <u>are</u>, <u>have</u>, <u>give</u>, <u>one</u>.

*a-e = Vowel-Consonant-<u>e</u>.

**This is a variance from <u>Webster's Dictionary</u> 2nd edition   <u>bâre</u>

V-e

Open Syllable	Closed Syllable	VCe
no ———————	not ———————	note
by	bit	bite
so	sol	sole
me	met	mete
I	id	ide
a	at	ate

---

r may slightly alter the preceding vowel sound.		u after l, r, s:	
bare	flare	plume	assume
cure	here	prune	intrude
sire	care	rude	capsule

Final (k) after a long vowel:

cock	coke	tack	take
smock	smoke	pick	pike
duck	duke	tick	tike
snack	snake	stock	stoke

Final e is silent.

tense	glimpse	impulse
solve	collapse	ellipse

V-e̱

Open Syllable		Closed Syllable		VCe̱	Final e̱ is silent
ho	-	hop	-	hope	babe
my	-	mill	-	mile	bare
sly	-	slid	-	slide	yoke
no	-	nod	-	node	fuss
a	-	add	-	ade	lyre
spy	-	spit	-	spite	prose
lo	-	lop	-	lope	spume
pry	-	prim	-	prime	clove
a	-	Al	-	ale	brute
fly	-	flit	-	flite	rare
lo	-	lob	-	lobe	swale
try	-	trip	-	tripe	squire
spy	-	spin	-	spine	probe
lo	-	Lon	-	lone	flute
sly	-	slim	-	slime	style
spy	-	spill	-	spile	spare
lo	-	lot	-	lote	Ute
my	-	mit	-	mite	fife
hi	-	hid	-	hide	truce
by	-	bid	-	bide	tare
mu	-	miss	-	mice	sire
hi	-	hick	-	hike	grope
try	-	trick	-	trike	strafe
spy	-	spick	-	spike	scribe

bit	bite	pane	pan	twine	twin
cut	cute	rip	ripe	node	nod
cane	can	rate	rat	till	tile
fade	fad	rod	rode	tine	tin
fat	fate	Sal	sale	tripe	trip
grip	gripe	slop	slope	van	vane
gal	gale	slime	slim	tot	tote
hope	hop	tame	tam	dude	dud
hid	hide	time	Tim	bane	ban
kit	kite	tap	tape	lam	lame
Jane	Jan	type	tip	spin	spine
Lon	lone	tube	tub	lope	lop
Lyn	line	wine	win	cube	cub
mad	made	yipe	yip	cop	cope
mane	man	strip	stripe	din	dine
mat	mate	ale	Al	trode	trod
mull	mule	Dan	Dane	gate	gat
mode	mod	dam	dame	mal	male
robe	rob	fill	file	cod	code
mitt	mite	gape	gap	cape	cap
mope	mop	fine	fin	dole	doll
nape	nap	hat	hate	dun	dune
note	not	rim	rime	dote	dot
pin	pine	ride	rid	grade	grad
pale	pal	sit	site	spite	spit

plane	plan	pleb	plebe
quit	quite	glad	glade
prime	prim	game	gam
sin	sine	grim	grime
style	still	bide	bid
sol	sole	jape	Jap
Sam	same	slid	slide
rot	rote	flit	flite
pip	pipe	muse	muss
glime	glim	sate	sat
mim	mime	cad	cade
pope	pop	met	mete
scrap	scrape	tome	Tom
bate	bat	ode	odd
at	ate	Ross	rose
use	us	mome	mom
glob	globe	vale	Val
tide	tid	pat	pate
cote	cot	slat	slate
snip	snipe	Pete	pet
fane	fan	Sid	side
lobe	lob	jute	jut
con	cone	Moll	mole
mute	mutt	wan	wane
dim	dime	wad	wade

V-e

stack	-	stake	coke	-	cock
Jake	-	Jack	pick	-	pike
smock	-	smoke	crake	-	crack
quake	-	quack	snack	-	snake
stoke	-	stock	tike	-	tick
slack	-	slake	back	-	bake
duke	-	duck	Luke	-	luck
tack	-	take	moke	-	mock
poke	-	pock	block	-	bloke

hiss	-	hike	-	hick
sake	-	sack	-	sass
rack	-	race	-	rake
truck	-	truce	-	truss
mike	-	mice	-	miss
pass	-	pace	-	pack
like	-	lice	-	lick
Dick	-	dice	-	dike
brake	-	brace	-	brass
trick	-	trice	-	trike

bass	back	base	bake
lack	lace	lass	lake
mace	Mack	make	mass

nick - nice   slick - slice   track - trace

* *

hace	sone	plunce	clape
ruce	trast	hape	clapse
runce	buke	hapse	scred
sep	lig	lut	plime
bute	nide	stete	spule
flad	crem	pribe	spulse
vene	jole	scote	og
hile	scon	trab	cime
gult	hume	stull	bince
gulse	labe	vule	bix
gune	stince	kyx	cline
nate	stig	zote	spone
nup	pede	fract	zome
voke	slox	loff	sug
wole	slote	stume	fep
het	sape	frig	frime
spon	sile	cobe	milse
lete	silse	cile	rybe
lype	smig	syme	gure
dran	wape	tulse	grune
sote	stute	cine	lun
dopse	plag	plene	gace
clin	spuss	bune	gance
fraz	plun	cise	smole

accuse	landscape	Blackstone
admire	incense	sincere
complete	combine	compute
confuse	explode	advise
dissolve	invite	compete
costume	velvet	fixate
custom	dispute	distance
arrive	enclose	immune
concrete	umpire	insane
pancake	compose	bandit
escape	sunrise	explore
trombone	condole	entire
expense	nonsense	excuse
stampede	baptize	translate
exile	capsule	Gladstone
advice	glassware	ignite
inside	endure	injure
ignore	symptom	involve
suspense	excite	invade
suppose	dictate	connote
trumpet	backbone	impose
tadpole	extreme	entrance
empire	compare	banquet
reptile	system	expose
collapse	instance	inspire

vampire	entice	textile
consume	attic	obscure
collide	quagmire	commune
immense	gangrene	sublime
exhume	convene	pulsate
convince	excrete	obtuse
illume	condone	extrude
confide	conclude	ensconce
console	comprise	obscene
pollute	mantis	narrate
dispose	entwine	obtrude
alcove	excise	transmute
expire	membrane	syndrome
esquire	hindrance	oppose
magnate	truncate	cosmos
magnet	impede	stagnate
Neptune	incite	stagnant
exhale	inscribe	octane
intense	ferrule	Vulgate
induce	enclave	suffice
ellipse	enzyme	convulse
cascade	garrote	ensnare
assume	invoke	concede
possum	impute	abstruse
empire	immure	cristate

connive

astute

compote

semblance

mandrake

contrive

pyrrole

contrite

commence

Klondike

conspire

adjure

henbane

muslin

entire

effuse

ferrite

hectare

advance

Essene

essence

muckrake

collude

oppose

embrace

lignite

imbibe

exclude

Pembroke

conduce

enhance

intrude

impulse

accede

allure

ampere

apprise

calcite

concise

pittance

adduce

benzene

expanse

Hellene

cognate

appose

allude

subsume

Stanhope

transcribe

compensate

concentrate

illustrate

confiscate

infiltrate

infantile

oscillate

contemplate

inculpate

impregnate

indispose

insensate

consummate

aggrandize

exsiccate

ambuscade

eglantine

intestate

hellandite

inculate

exculpate

scintillate

pistillate

hellgrammite

billinsgate

Kate's Sale

said   to   do   the
Mr.   Mrs.   Dr.

Kate said, "I must pick up my stuff as Mom said to do! My case is crammed, my box is filled, my stand is spilling, and my bed is hidden! At long last I must pick up, pack up, tuck in and fit in my stuff!"

Kate spent a long time picking up, packing up, tucking in and fitting in. Still, stuff was left.

"I will set it in a pile, since I can't use it, and sell it to my pals!"

Kate made and set up:

Kate planned to sell:

**Sat. P.M. Sale
at
Kate's Gate !**
2:00's the time. Bring a dime.

1. a rusty rake
2. a long rope
3. a big kite
4. a red robe
5. an odd bone

6. five plastic cubes
7. a brass bell
8. six pine cones
9. a sandbag frog
10. a cute black bug

Gals came. Lads came. Mr. and Mrs. Drake and Dr. Stone came. The sale was on!

Mr. Drake got the rake to use on his drive.

Tim Tope got the rope to spin and jump.

Ferris Fite had the big kite he wanted to fly.

Dr. Stone added the big bone to his lot.

Molly Mobe had pride in the soft red robe.

Tom Tubes fitted and stacked the five plastic cubes.

Dave Snell kept ringing his fat brass bell.

Jolly Jones sniffed his six pine cones.

Polly Wog hugged the sandbag frog and tossed it to Mrs. Drake.

But not a lad and not a lass wanted the cute black bug!

Kate wore a smile and said, "I do not care! I will tame it and name it Betsy. I will pet it and let it get snug on my rug.

Nine pals I thank – the sale was fine. 90¢ to the bank, but B. Bug's mine!"

The Bike Race

Rod rode on the back of the same bike as
Sam did in the race.
Bick set the pace, but he let the pack pass
him.

Smile Time

Jock can don his fake face, tell us jokes,
and use his cane as a wand.
Dick can try tricks on his trike and bike,
brace himself, and flip on a brass rod.
Dot dotes on a happy gang, so doles dolls
to bring smiles.

The Rascals

Al is glad to escape to the glade and drink
ale.
He spiles up the keg so not a drop escapes
and spills!
Val wins a toss, and skips off to sip wine
at the same spot in the vale.
A bloke lops off six carrots and lopes cross
the block fence!

A hick takes a plate of muffins and a fast hike.

But luckless Luke is nabbed as he rips off a ripe berry.

Must the cop use Mace to cope? No, it makes a mess.

And five rascals do not comprise a mob to stop!

Male Style

Wid is so wide, it must be his fate to be fat.

A sack is best in Wid's case, so he has a pink smock!

In the sake of style, jazzy Jess has flame-red flare pants.

Finn's duds are fine, and he likes to act like a dude!

Rob picks up robes, caps and capes, but hates hats!

Tim is quite mod in the mode of the time. To him, a tam is tame.

Adjusting the plume on his plum fez, he states, "A fad fades, but it's still fun!"

A Time of Life

Mr. Ross likes to muse on the past.
"The rose I save has lost its smell, but I
   am still impressed by it. I must not
   muss it!"
Miss Grace, in lace, drifts like a wan lass
   on the grass as the crescent wanes.
The odd ode Miss Grace intones by rote
   ends, "And red rocks run, and, running,
   rot!"

Pets and Pals

Pete and Sal and I take a pet to Mame's.
No sale is on. Pals on the block just strut
   and stroke pets.
Pete rubs his mongrel on the nape of the
   neck as it naps.
Pam's parrot sits on a pole and mocks
   Mack's moke. The ass backs off!
Slim's bunny hid in the slime and blinks at
   the sun.
Cal's angry cat takes licks at its lice and
   takes swats at its nits!
Mike has his mice race across a canvas cot.

Nell pens Miss Nanny in a cote.

Mad Jo has the job of tending to Moll's pet mole! "Ban moles!" he insists. "A mole is the bane of my life! It makes humps and clips bulbs."

Mel's mule mulls the fate of Kent's cock as it hops into a crate. It can't sip Coke!

Mr. Stripe, Sid's snake, rates bits of rat, bits of frog, and strips of bat as snacks on the side!

The sun is hot, so Betty's cub sits close to the big ice cubes to sate himself.

Mr. Mute, Sally's yelling mutt, got a scare as he slid on the slide, so we hug him.

And we quake at the quack of Duke's ducks on the pond!

 Explore More!

Explode a rocket into space?
Ignore insane advice!
Twelve capsules up? I must conclude
MY planning can't suffice!

Men!

Kate: Nick is nice to his pals AND to gals like us.

Cat: Dick makes up dice games we can use.

Kate: Ken can cut a fancy rug!

Cat: Van is as cute as a cock on a vane!

Kate: Hume can strum the tunes Sis hums him.

Cat: Mack makes fun of us and makes me mad!

Kate: Moke can mock and ape the men on TV.

Cat: Hal is hale and hip!

Kate: Lyn has quite a line!

Cat: If Lon were the lone man left, I'd run!

Kate: But if Sol were the sole man left, I'd flip!

Cat: Sis's dates are fun to discuss!

Kate: Yes! Let's gossip more!

<u>Tell</u> <u>It</u> <u>As</u> <u>It</u> (ĭz)

Jack and I went off to Camp Spruce last June. He was my best pal. He passed notes to me at sack time. I handed him notes back, stuck into his cot blanket. If Big Lad came by past Taps time, it was tense. But if a lad in the tent got a glimpse of a note, he was not wise to it. No one else but me was to solve Jack's notes. No one else but Jack was to solve mine.

Here is Jack's last note to me.

(hī)(tĭm)!
(thē)(năp)(bī)(thē)(lōn)(pĭn)(ŏn)(thē)
(slōp)(wŏz)(fŭn)!
(ĭn)(thē)(kămp)(gāmz)(ī)(wĭl)(tōs)(ā)
[plāt](dĭs´kŭs), (jŭmp)(thē)(stĭk)(ŏn)(thē)
[pōl], (ănd)(hŏp)(ĭn)(thē)(săk)(rās). (kwĭk´lĭ̯
(ī)(hōp)!   (tĭl)(nĕkst)(tĭm), (jăk)

75

reckless	fondness	jestful
stripless	stillness	glassful
restless	sadness	primly
stringless	gladness	madly
lately	pipeful	blameless
safely	useful	timeless
namely	faceful	styleless
finely	grateful	careless
closely	fateful	tireless
gamely	graceful	smileless
merely	caseful	hopeless
rarely	baneful	nameless
nicely		
tamely	cures	wiseness
purely	mules	cuteness
ripely	tomes	paleness
stately	tykes	tameness
completely	piles	muteness

Running Time

Trucks run well a long time on
tubeless tires.
TV sets kept on a long time run on
tireless tubes!

Mad, Sad, Glad

Mom: Galloping gallumpus – I am going to pop my top!!! Home has gotten to be a mess – a disgraceful place, and it's gotten <u>to</u> me! I want assistance! But I have the best gang of males in Texas. I hope Dad and the lads sense my unhappy state. H-m-m-m-m. If I extend snacks, I bet the job will get done! I'll give a hint –

CRACK!!
BANG!!
SPLAT!!

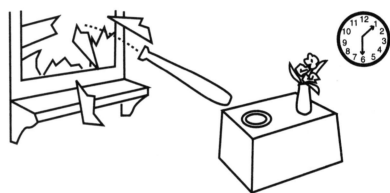

Dan: I lost my grip as I hit, and the bat got tossed and landed here. I bet Dad will gripe and give me a spanking!

Dad: No licks, Jack! But do not just gape at the gap and hope the pane will fix itself! Grab a pan, pick up the glass and dispose of the bits in the big can. Hop to it!

Mom: As long as the dust pan is here, can we make a plan and lessen the mess in this place? A snack is in the offing if it's spic and span by 3:00.

Si: O.K.! Let's pick jobs and "get on the stick!"

Mom: Fine! I'll go bake a cake and be back!

Sid: I'll collect the scraps and scrape up the mud here. I can trace the tracks my sandals made!

Dan: I'll get the mop and wipe up the spot on the mat the vase fell on.

Dane: I'll get my socks from spin dry, mate them, and set the pile by the mending kit. I wore holes in five socks!

Si: I'll stack the tent stakes and pile the canvas.

Sid: I'll hang the rake on the rack.

Dan: I'll stock a pile of sticks and stoke it in the fire place.

Dad: I'll tape the dripping tap and fix the fuse so I can't fuss!

Dane: I'll wipe off the big globe in the den. The glob of jam I dropped on it blotted Scotland and hid Ireland!

Si: I plan to give back the plane Cliff gave me – it broke!

Sid: I'll take the snaps of the babes back to Babs. Cass is a case, and Gale is quite a gal!

Dan: I'll take the twin tots a gift I made from a packing crate. I must cut a bit of twine and string it in the holes so the tykes can tote and drag it.

 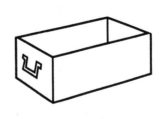

Dane: It will make a cute truck!

Si: I'll get a strip of plastic to fill the empty space the bat made.

Sid: I'll bring the tape and help apply it to the frame.

Dan: O.K.! I'll have to crack my piggy bank and use $5.00 to get us the next pane!

Dane: I'll tip the type and dust Jack's desk.

Si: I'll mend Jake's singing top. The jut in its jute string makes it spin on its spine, not its tip.

Sid: I'll set Mom's potted plants by the stile on the fence.

Dan: I'll give Bon his bone by the stile. He can slop on the slope, not the rug, since he's still a puppy!

Dane: The grime was grim.

Si: But I mope if I have to mop up!

Sid: It tires me to do tasks, but it's fun to complete a job.

Dad: Can we solve the problem of mess so Mom will not get so upset the next time?

Dan: I'd best be more careful as I bat! It costs plenty if I'm not!

Dane: I'd best snack on a plate and napkin!

Si: We can store the camping stuff in the next empty crate we get from a store.

Sid: It can save us time is we scrape on the mat as we get home.

Mom: It is 3:00 on the dot. Did we make it?

Dan: Inspect us, Mom!

Mom: Getting command of the mess we had takes a lot of grit. I commend my men – it's spotless! Here's a Fuzzy Fizz and the snack I made.

Dane: It's nice to get a pat on the back –

Si: and a glad mom –

Sid: **and** a yummy hot cake!

O, Nonsense!

Mr. Slox wore a Stetson on his funny,
    glunny locks.
And a plonce on his pants, and a quome,
And he ate glate collix from a treppy,
    dreppy box,
As he strockened on a docken to his home.

Mr. Slox had a mastiff by his zilly-zally
    zome,
As he drabbened on a grabben-like gate.
"If I tire, I expire, so to pobby dobby dome
Ride I mastiff till it's lingot longot late!"

91,92

crudely	lameness	scares
closeness	yokeless	stateless
tuneful	jokeful	wireless
flameless	sanely	pureness
apes	drakes	spares
sameness	bales	barely
gravely	zoneless	prideful
wakeful	plateful	iceless
traceless	rudeness	scopes
scribes	homely	squareness
lonely	timely	widely
bruteful	wideness	glides
lateness	careful	glareless
scoreless	spiceless	hopeful
Utes	wares	safeness
soreness	staleness	bladeless
lively	wifely	wisely
dareless	viceful	stareful
crateful	boneless	trades
lures	jibes	bareness
fumeless	priceless	solely
niceness	blameful	voteless
doleful	fakeness	loneness
swipes	bravely	quoteful
squarely	cranes	dales

hats	capless	quakeful
hates	capes	quakes
hateless	capful	quackless
hatful	capeless	quacks
hateful	caps	quakeless
hatless	tubs	likely
fadeless	tubes	likes
fadful	tubless	licks
fadless	tubeful	likeness
fades	tubeless	lickless
fadeful	tubful	dimeless
fads	gripeful	dimness
planes	gripless	dimly
planless	grips	dims
plans	gripeless	dimes
planeful	gripes	rimless
planless	gripful	rimeless
spiteless	rackless	rimes
spites	rakes	rimeful
spits	rackful	rims
spiteful	rakeless	tapeless
spitless	rakeful	tapeful
robes	racks	taps
robs	spiles	tapes
robeless	spills	tapless

Mom is happy if Sis sings a song nicely.
Dad is likely to clap time if the song is tuneful.
Ron merely stands by with a smileless face.
And I am just grateful as it stops!

It was purely luck as Mel stole home safely.
The rest of the lads did bravely but lost the
 game.
Not a smile on the doleful Dallas Dudes!
But the sadness cannot last long.
Try more next time, gang!

Tad made the kite completely stringless and
 stripless on his bed.
The robeless tot ran to mom and sobbed, "I'm
 sorry!"
His cuteness was useful to his excuse.

Stately Cassy Cat sniffs twice and blinks primly.
Prideful Cassy scoffs at the nameless tomcat
 and wisely strides past him.

As Dad sat by the fire, restless Tim got him his mules and a pipeful.

Dad was jestful to Tim and gave him useful advice: Do as I tell, not as I do!

Sam got a scare at sunset – a caveful of bats!

A paleness came to his face as dimness came in the sky.

The track was the same here as here as here!

Sam was lost in the sameness and lonely in the stillness.

But help came in time as his dog, Rags, trotted up.

Rags gave him a faceful of licks and led him to the track home.

Sam was grateful to his priceless pet!

The dog sped a mile on the track of the reckless rabbit.

The rabbit escapes safely into an end of his tunnel.

The dog gapes gravely at the empty hole – a timeless tale of wit and wiseness!

Mom and Mel went to The Pants Place.
It is hopeless to get Mel to pick fast.
At last Mom got him black slacks to try on
from the rackful.

Dive in, lads, it's snack time!
Fill up on a glassful of milk and a plateful of cake.

A cat got careless and went up to a nest.
It rarely happens, but the cat had a bad time.
The redwing on the eggs got hateful and spiteful.
Dive, hit, cling, swat, peck!
Careful, cat!
Next time a fateful attack can happen!

Br-r-r-r-r! Br-r-r-r-r!
At 20? A frameful of finely-made mist, a
paneful of closely-made frost,
and a pileful of mutely-made flakes!

Clumsy Cal is my best pal,
But Graceful Greg will get the gal!

SPOT THE ODD

Read each line and decide which word is unlike the others in meaning.

1. gulf   pond   lake   <u>luck</u>

2. rice   lice   mites   ticks

3. Pete   Kate   Clyde   Hank

4. clams   mules   mussels   crabs

5. wallop   swipe   strike   bike

6. grapes   plugs   plums   figs

7. spit   lick   like   suck

8. fret   mope   fuss   fuse

9. mice   race   rats   moles

10. clap   grab   wave   snore

11. dent   plume   crack   bend

12. cup   cake   mug   glass

13. dolls   tops   kites   mops

14. gallon   elm   aspen   pine

SPOT THE ODD

Read each line and decide which word is unlike the others in meaning.

1. doll   top   <u>pot</u>   kite
2. run   gallop   trot   rote
3. slope   dill   hill   dune
4. jibs   kids   jests   jibes
5. vest   robe   rest   dress
6. zips   putts   buttons   snaps
7. wink   stare   blink   strict
8. skull   spine   stone   bone
9. cap   tame   tam   hat
10. twine   wine   string   rope
11. possum   rabbit   skunk   snake
12. poles   stakes   stacks   spikes
13. sing   yell   hum   bend
14. base   bat   mutt   mitt

LEVEL III

Preparation:

Much practice in reading and spelling VrrV and Vre words. <u>carry</u> <u>care</u>

Explanation of Vr:

r CONTROLS THE SOUND OF A PRECEDING VOWEL WHEN:
  1. r FALLS BEFORE ANY CONSONANT EXCEPT ANOTHER r
  2. r IS FINAL IN A WORD

Otherwise, the vowel before r behaves as it does before any other consonant (although r may slightly alter the long or short sound).

The dictionary shows (ûr) in accented syl. and (ẽr) in unaccented syl. Both sound pictures have the same pronunciation, and the diacritical marks are unimportant except for helping the student to recognize and pronounce (ûr) and (ẽr) when he meets them in the dictionary.

Since Level I, the student has been dividing between two r's which behave as any other double con. and causes the preceding vowel to be short. <u>berry</u> <u>urr</u> words are exceptions. The dictionary assigns (ûr) markings rather than (ŭr). However, the two sounds are so similar that the exception causes no problem. <u>hurry</u>

In Level II, the student treated final silent <u>e</u> after a vowel and an r just as he treated any other VCe situation. <u>here</u>   <u>endure</u>   <u>fire</u>

IN THIS LEVEL, THE STUDENT LEARNS WHEN r DOES CHANGE A VOWEL SOUND.

In the next level (Level IV, dividing words with Vowel-Con.-Vowel pattern), words with Vr + another vowel will be treated just as any other VCV word. The vowel before r is long, short, etc., just as it would be before any other con. r does not usually control a previous vowel sound in a base word if it is followed by another vowel. <u>he´ro</u>   <u>ver´y</u>

Page	Letter Order	Concepts to Develop

<u>er</u>, <u>ir</u>, <u>ur</u> (ûr) (ẽr): Since the sound pictures are pronounced the same, the ANGLING workbook suggests that in the exercises the student simply places a circumflex ^ over accented (ûr) <u>hêr</u> <u>cûr</u> <u>fîr</u>, and a tilde ˜ over unaccented (ẽr) <u>banker</u>

93   er (ûr) (ẽr)   For Reading:
                              er = (ûr) (ẽr)
                                1. at end of word <u>her</u>
                                2. before any consonant except another r <u>herd</u>
                                   <u>er</u> (ẽr) suffix
                          For Spelling:
                              <u>er</u> (ur) is the only regular spelling response,
                              except after <u>w</u> (See <u>wor</u>)

90

96   ur (ûr)

For Reading:
  <u>ur</u> = (ûr) before any consonant or when final in a word. <u>cur</u> <u>turtle</u>
For Spelling: Irregular

97   ir (ûr)

For Reading:
  <u>ir</u> = (ûr)
    1. at end of a word   <u>fir</u>
    2. before any consonant except another <u>r</u>   <u>bird</u>
      one common exception   <u>squirrel</u>
For Spelling: Irregular

100   or (ôr) (ẽr)

For Reading:
  <u>or</u> = (ôr)
    1. in final accented syl.   <u>for</u>
    2. before any consonant except another <u>r</u>   <u>bôrder</u>
      EXCEPTION: in final unaccented syl. <u>oxford</u>
                                  <u>stubborn</u>
  <u>or</u> = (ẽr) in final unaccented syl.   <u>doctor</u>
  <u>or</u> (ẽr) suffix
For Spelling: <u>or</u> (ẽr) Irregular

100   wor (wûr)

For Spelling:
  <u>wor</u> = regular spelling after <u>w</u>   <u>world</u>
Learned Word: <u>were</u>

102   ar (är) (ẽr)

For Reading:
  <u>ar</u> (är)
    1. in final accented syl.
    2. before any consonant except another <u>r</u>
      EXCEPTION: in final unaccented syl.   <u>inward</u>
                                    <u>braggart</u>
  <u>ar</u> (ẽr) in final unaccented syl.   <u>dollar</u>
For Spelling: <u>ar</u> (ẽr) Irregular

  <u>ar</u> after <u>w</u> and <u>qu</u> = (ôr)   <u>war</u>   <u>quart</u>
  In Level I, the student learned that <u>a</u> after <u>w</u> or after <u>qu</u> (kw) is usually (ŏ).   <u>watch</u>

  This is a parallel situation; however, the sounds (wär) and (wôr) are very similar and drill in distinguishing between the sounds is unnecessary since <u>wor</u> regular spells (wûr).

Page	Letter Order	Concepts to Develop (cont..)
115	g (j)	For Reading: g (j) before e, i, and y, USUALLY Spelling Situation: Initial and medial (j): Use g before e, i, and y; otherwise, use j EXCEPTION: syl. ject: reject subject
117	dge (j)	Trigraph: three letters making one sound For Reading: dge words: Delay final (j) spelling until initial and medial situation is thoroughly understood and automatic Spelling Situation: Use dge at the end of a one-syl. word after a short vowel; otherwise use ge English basewords do not end in j or je age (ĭj) is a base word ending and a suffix. Final age (ĭj) is regular for reading and spelling. Final (ĭj) in multisyllable words = age.

Consonant Digraphs: Review definition of term. Digraph = two letters making one sound. (Digraph letters stick together and act as one con. in syl. division.)
mar shal

Page	Letter Order	Concepts to Develop (cont..)
119	sh (sh)	
121	ch (ch) (k) (sh)	Irregular for spelling (k) and (sh)
124	tch (ch)	Trigraph Spelling Situation: Use tch at the end of a one-syl. word after a short vowel; otherwise, use ch. EXCEPTIONS: which rich such much These are learned words.
125	th (th) (th)	Final e after th makes the V. long and the th voiced. cloth clothe Learned word: there
127	wh (hw)	Discriminate between w (lip shaping) and wh (blowing). wha may be (hwŏ) or (hwă). what wham Learned Words: who whose whom where
130	ph (f)	For Spelling: Irregular Spelling Rule: Words ending in s, x, z, ch and sh spell their plurals by adding es. Third person singular verbs follow same rule. He passes. es adds an extra syl. to these words. boxes benches Adding s to words ending in ce and ge adds an extra syl. laces cages

er (ûr) (ẽr)

fern	concert	stutter	mercy
terse	holler	verdict	perfect
nerve	linger	cistern	manner
verse	luster	scamper	dinner
yerk	mutter	concern	differ
serve	number	ferment	expert
pert	pattern	hinder	fluster
bern	rafter	dagger	banner
swerve	scatter	amber	fender
jerk	center	confer	hammer
her	cluster	hamster	jabber
term	cancer	filter	butler
herd	glimmer	perhaps	blunder
stern	after	plaster	lantern
verb	lobster	servant	letter
erse	bitter	pester	limber
erst	cinder	slipper	latter
	finger	temper	perfume
pamper	permit	otter	clabber
hermit	fritter	Vermont	termite
flatter	kernel	western	culvert
butter	offer	yonder	vesper
copper	ponder	sterling	person
Buster	sermon	perspire	lumber
Denver	observe	gangster	derby

udder	dexter	persist	jumper
umber	fervent	advert	killer
percent	glister	blubber	passer
otter	inverse	convert	picker
ulcer	censer	canker	printer
monster	fervid	cistern	renter
prosper	lectern	discern	sifter
lancer	pincers	obverse	stinger
plunder	perplex	spencer	welder
clatter	spinster	excerpt	filler
ember	vertex	Herbert	**Suffix er: more than**
assert	twitter	commerce	faster
berserk	tumbler	converce	blacker
bluster	sternum	scepter	longer
cruller	verbose	scunner	stronger
immerce	smatter	conserve	softer
adverb	swelter	**Suffix er: one who, that which**	stiffer
perjure	vermin	banker	swifter
pervade	utter	blocker	lesser
proffer	squander	kicker	duller
aster	verdant	bumper	pinker
roster	Antwerp	camper	sicker
serpent	versus	drifter	stricter
jerkin	ulster	hanger	blunter
adverse	smelter	golfer	fonder

94

er

er (ûr)

  1. at end of word: - - - -   her

  2. before any consonant
     except another r   - - - -   herd, hermit

er (ĕr)

  before another r   - - - -   hĕrring

er (ēr)

  in final e-r-e   - - - -   hēre

* * * * * * * * * * * * * * * * * * * *

spler	derse	kert	slere
splere	derrin	kere	slern
splern	der	kerron	slerrip
terro	blerk	vern	flerse
tert	blere	ver	flerron
ter	blerric	verrot	flere
plere	glerst	zere	swer
pler	glerro	zerst	swere
plerris	glere	zerret	swerrot

95

<u>ur</u> (ûr) (ẽr)

urn	burst	burly	gurglet
purse	spurt	incur	purflin
fur	turf	absurd	curvet
curve	burse	turban	turbit
cur	spur	turnip	burbod
curb	purr	surprise	furtive
burn	curt	flurry	gurnet
blur	durst	burlap	furfur
burg	furze	curtsy	furcate
blurt	furl	nurture	turnix
curl	murk	cursive	turbid
spurn	curr	sturdy	surmise
Turk	hurt	surplus	Turco
surf	purl	turnstile	urban
burr	curst	disturb	urbane
curse	curn	survive	turbot
hurds	burnt	nocturn	ursine
scurf	burl	Burmese	purpure
lurk	slur	disburse	current
surd		curry	Hapsburg
turn	burden	nocturne	turret
nurse	occur	burnet	scurry
hurl	concur	perturb	longspur
curd	murder	purser	Homburg
burp	murmur	curtate	burro

ir (ûr)

bird	flirt	firman
mir	quirk	firkin
irk	twirl	circlet
fir	skirt	confirm
sir	smirk	kirkman
dirt	first	kirmess
stir	swirl	hircine
girl	spirt	hirsute
gird	birse	virgule
kirk	skirl	birling
firm	stirk	virgate
mirk	squirt	Sterling
pirn	squirm	firstling
dirl	stirps	
birl		circumflex
girn	Virgo	circumvent
tirl	Irwin	circumfuse
girt	circus	circumspect
yird	zircon	circumvolve
dirk	Irving	circumstance
kirn	affirm	circumscribe
birk	girder	circumvallate
virl	infirm	

ir

ir (ûr) (ẽr)
  1. at end of word: - - - -   sir
  2. before any consonant
     except another r   - - - -   bird, circus

ir (ĭr)
  before another r
  (except: squirrel)   - - - -   cĭrrus

ir (īr)
  in final i-r-e   - - - -   fīre

* *

nir	smirt	blirk	flirp
nirron	smirro	blirrel	flirro
nire	smire	blire	flire
glire	bire	stird	slire
glirt	birrop	stire	slirn
glirret	birm	stirro	slirret
snirrem	pirt	plirk	zire
snire	pire	plirrid	zirrex
snirp	pirrit	plire	zirp
skirn	kirm	dwirrep	clir
skirrem	kire	dwire	clire
skire	kirrel	dwirl	clirrid

<u>or</u> (ôr)

1. in accented syl. at end of word
2. before any consonant except another r (unless in final unaccented syl.)

fork	corm	afford	accord
for	orc	assort	orbit
nor	orb	border	absorb
torte	York	ornate	orlon
born	kor	distort	Morgan
cord	bort	export	bornite
cork	corse	forceps	morsel
fort	dorm	hormone	bordel
forte	ford	endorse	sordid
horn	corf	morbid	rorqual
horse	corpse	torment	ormer
sort	force	mortal	cordite
storm	lorn	escort	dormer
stork	mort	ordnance	extort
morn	gorse	dormant	gorcock
lord	port	enforce	fornix
corn	horst	forlorn	torpid
snort	horde	Jordan	torsade
form	dorp	Mormon	formyl
scorn	orle	Hortense	hornet
norm	dorr	torso	orcin
pork	torsk	vortex	ordure
sorb	ort	Waldorf	orlop

or (ẽr)

or (ẽr): in final unaccented syl.

doctor	proctor	**wor (wûr)**
horror	pallor	
pastor	Suffix or: one who, that which	world
scissors	error	wort
sculptor	actor	work
splendor	bettor	worm
sponsor		worse
terror	conductor	word
tractor	instructor	worst
victor	investor	
rector	successor	worry
fervor	contractor	worsen
candor	inventor	ribwort
captor	inspector	madwort
censor	confessor	dropwort
mentor	objector	worsted
torpor	possessor	borwort
harbor	compressor	muckworm
succor	aggressor	bellwort
sector	tormentor	glasswort
cantor	inductor	
castor	oppressor	trelliswork
sceptor	transgressor	
rancor	collector	

or

or (ôr)
  1. in unaccented syl. at end of word - - - - fôr

  2. before any consonant except
     another r (unless in final
     unaccented syl.) - - - - fôrk, ôrder

or (ẽr)
  in final unaccented syl. - - - - doctõr

or (ŏr)
  before another r - - - - sŏrry

or (ōr)
  in final o-r-e - - - - sōre

* * * * * * * * * * * * * * * * * * *

clor	vor	zor
clort	vorse	zorp
clorgo	vornic	zordon
clańtor	vesˊtor	zeńdor
clorren	vorry	zorret
clore	vore	zore
slor	quor	gror
slorg	quorse	grorn
slorlid	quorgo	grorsel
slańgor	quaffor	gruˊsor
slorrip	quorret	grorrig
slore	quore	grore

<u>ar</u> (är) ☆

1. in accented syl. at end of word
2. before any consonant except another <u>r</u> (unless in final unaccented syl.)

star	tart	army	largo
hard	snarl	carbine	marlin
arm	spar	darling	carbide
barb	marl	carbon	arctic
arc	park	garlic	carcass
cart	art	cargo	marmot
carte	gar	garment	varlet
darn	lard	carpet	garner
garb	spark	garter	ardent
bark	yarn	hardly	marvel
carve	mar	harness	harbor
dart	lark	jargon	parlance
harm	dark	harvest	sarcasm
scarp	harp	market	margrave
scar	Marx	pardon	arbor
tarn	marc	parlor	larkspur
smart	scart	parcel	marlite
starve	nard	martyr	Spartan
yard	mart	parsnip	marmite
hark	scarf	scarlet	garden
bard	start	tardy	Harlem
ark	dwarf	starling	tartrate
par	stark	garnet	armure

ar (ẽr)

ar (ẽr) in final unaccented syllable		Suffix ward: direction toward; tendency to
dollar	blizzard	backward
collar	drunkard	inward
cellar	gizzard	landward
beggar	mallard	onward
grammar	scabbard	upward
hangar	custard	westward
pillar	mustard	windward
burglar	standard	forward
bursar	buzzard	afterward
mortar	haggard	homeward
nectar	laggard	**ar (ôr)**
poplar	niggard	after w and qu
tartar	sluggard	war
vulgar	tankard	warn
stellar	dastard	wart
pedlar	halyard	swarm
templar	lanyard	quart
palmar	lombard	quartz
lascar	Hansard	warfare
plantar	mozzard	warden
Oscar	gurnard	quartet
bulwark	gabbard	quartile
braggart	izzard	quarter

ar

ar (är)
1. in unaccented syl. at end of word - - - - stär

2. before any consonant except
another r (unless in final
unaccented syl.) - - - - stärt, därling

ar (ẽr)
in final unaccented syl. - - - - dollãr

ar (ăr)
before another r - - - - mărry

ar (ār)
in final a-r-e - - - - cāre

* *

smar	clar	plar
smarn	clard	plarst
smargo	clarsen	plarby
smennar	contar	plissar
smarry	clarren	plarrot
smare	clare	plare
larg	yar	sar
lartic	yarl	sare
lunnar	yarlet	sarfon
larrem	yempar	sebbar
lare	yarret	sarress

Confusing Words

silt	snug	curst	salve
slit	sung	crust	slave
form	sang	crate	stirps
from	snag	carte	strips
crave	nest	spilt	strave
carve	nets	split	starve
grist	clasp	lisp	crops
grits	claps	lips	corpse
lest	Strat	burnt	except
lets	start	brunt	expect
tort	grit	bran	assent
trot	girt	barn	accent
tarp	dart	grin	crusty
trap	drat	girn	curtsy
best	kist	drop	filter
bets	kits	dorp	flitter
cast	Bart	scarp	excerpt
cats	brat	scrap	expert
gird	grab	bard	conserve
grid	garb	brad	converse
	grad	drab	

er, ir, ur, ar, or

organdy
embargo
inferno
internal
ancestor
fervency
Normandy
imposter
abnormal
informal
Anderson
immortal
incarnate
kilderkin
important
surmullet
persimmon
Irvington
sarcastic
nocturnal
Limburger
butterfly
extirpate
hamburger
opportune

Jefferson
September
bombardon
Parnassus
intercept
suspender
antarctic
Arlington
advertise
Amsterdam
carpenter
surrender
pimpernel
interrupt
narcissus
intercede
expurgate
importune
interlude
ambergris
Axminster
intersect
Turkestan
cofferdam
interfere

hinterland
misfortune
carnallite
taskmaster
clodhopper
gormandize
peppermint
Birmingham
mercantile
martingale
turpentine
Burlington
transistor
wanderlust
discursive
intersperse
quarterback
scuppernong
perspective
Westminster
frankfurter
blunderbuss
smorgasbord
Switzerland
compartment

V<u>r</u>

topsy-turvy   carpetbagger
hurdy-gurdy   kindergarten
hurly-burly   quartermaster

* * * * * * * * * * * * * * * * * * * *

flerp	murst	circon	lerry
expere	suppare	dispire	tarrel
dirrel	vorrate	dermist	burdel
fure	exire	kerrin	cargate
turbil	dorsan	wirrep	birry
jare	quirrem	bork	commure
darp	narrop	torrin	cirbo
larrot	innare	parrate	comtere
nerton	darmos	varto	plirt
berro	dar	lirret	rire
exure	ferril	gure	querret

The <u>Snirp</u>

The Snirp was snippy, the Snirp was mad.
He swirled and stomped and lirruped a lad!

He smirked and sniffed and spilled a glirt.
He spanked a pirrel and dirrexed in dirt!

After his flirpon, he birked in mire,
Twirruped a twabber and slept by the fire!

The Twin Tots

Ned and Fred's mom will attend a party.
A sitter must come for her twin tots.
Ned and Fred's mom gets the help of the
    twin girls up the block.
Fran and Nan tend Fred and Ned from six
    till past the time for bed.

Ned's empty tummy hurts.
Nan gets him a snack.

    Fred has pangs in his tummy.
    Fran gets him bits and bites.

Ned wants a drink.
Nan gets him dark pop from a jug.

    Fred wants to wet his lips.
    Fran gets him a pink drink in a glass.

Ned gets restless.
Nan and Ned tug on a rope.

    Fred gets wiggly.
    Fran and Fred do jumping jacks.

Nan said, "I like - - -
    filling up my fat bank pig,
    and setting Dolly Polly's wig."

Ned said, "I like - - -
    sipping milk from a copper mug,
    and turning flip-flops on the rug."

Fran said, "I like - - -
    resting under the big lone pine,
    and sending notes to pals of mine."

Fred said, "I like - - -
    hitting on a fine big drum,
    and puffing up a wad of gum!"

Nan said, "I dislike - - -
    pepper dropped on top of eggs,
    and socks slip-slipping on my legs!"

Ned said, "I do not like - - -
    going to bed if the sun's still up,
    or picking up after my bad pup!"

Fran said, "I dislike - - -
    getting into the tub at nine,
    and doing backbends hurts my spine!"

Fred said, "I do not like - - -
    bumping my trike on the big fir's
    trunk, or mom's dubbing rocks I
    collect just JUNK."

Ned gets dusty.
Nan gets him to a sink.

    Fred gets dirty.
    Fran gets him to scrub up.

Ned wants a song.
Nan sings him a funny song.

    Fred wants a tune.
    Fran hums him a happy tune.

Ned wants a tale.
Nan tells him of the rabbit and the hare,.

    Fred wants a tale.
    Fran tells him of the fox and the grapes.

Ned wants a sitting game.
Nan gets him to tell his likes and dislikes.

Fred wants a restful game.
Fran gets him to tell <u>his</u> likes and
  dislikes.

After telling likes and dislikes,
  the lads and girls sit close.
After hugs and pats, the tots trot off to bed.

It is late as Ned and Fred's mom turns into
  the drive.
Nan and Fran rise from resting.
The girls had blinked off as the lads had
  bunked in.

Twin tots can tire big girls just lots!

Match word in left column with synonym in right column.

lass .	. bunked in
spine .	. care for
tend .	. dusty
slept .	. girl
dirty .	. blink
drink .	. sip
wink .	. song
tune .	. back
glass .	. mug

THE ERROR

Sir Percy Morgan
Lord Gordon Hortence

Sir Percy: Morgan, let us make a plan, man,
  For a party by the by.
I have asked Lord Gordon Jordon
  And his sister. We must try
To impress her! Ask the vintner,
  Mister Curtis, for fine wine.
Make a place on staff for Hortence,
  For her help is fast and fine.

Morgan: I will do just as you order.
  Yes, Sir Percy Quincy Quirk,
We will serve Lord Gordon Jordon
  And his sister, Jasmin Jerk,
As is fitting for a magnate
  In the garment industry.
For his sis, a sparkling spinster,
  Best of butlers I will be!

Lord Gordon: The estate here is quite splendid.
  O, the stunning, long expanse!
'Tis perturbing Sis got ill and had
  No warning in advance!
I will contemplate the gardens
  And the verdant, well-trimmed grass
And the elms with birds of scarlet –
  It's a glimpse I can't surpass!

Sir Percy: I will miss her, but implore you
  In the words you utter well.
To describe what you observe here
  And to her my offer tell:
Quincy Quarters has a master,
  (For my granddad's will was grand!)
But its distaff side is missing,
  So I'm asking Jasmin's hand!

crack   splat   clunk   plop

Hortence: Six glass goblets went berserk and
  Sterling platters fell, and corks
On the Burgundy went popping
  In the pantry, hurling forks!
Mercy me! The din and clatter!
  It's still startling as can be.
Corn and yams got on the carpet –
  Aspic splattered sink and me!

Lord Gordon: Butterfingers – we're conversing!
  My stern anger you've incurred.
You have triggered off my ulcer.
  (Jasmin Jerk gets MORE perturbed!)

Sir Percy: You, no more my fervent servants,
  Murmur madly, stand and cry!
Keep an upper lip that's stiff! In
  Adverse circumstance we TRY!

Morgan:	Princess Purr went after kippers.
	But the plate of turnips fell.
	Next the fancy gander tottered,
	And the dumpling plate as well!
Hortence:	It was just a silly error.
	For Purr's supper was forgot.
	Do affirm CAT as the culprit.
	And we beg, dismiss US not!
Sir Percy:	My surprise! Well, back to normal!
	Let's forget and not distort.
	We'll discuss important matters –
	Let me formally escort!
	Yes, my harmless, darling Burmese
	Begs a pardon. Let's not starve!
	Hortence, Morgan, serve the parsnips
	And the pork plate – I will carve!

GOSSIP Has It - - - !

From Miss Tidbit to Miss Smatt'ring to
    Miss Speck and to Miss Dot,
Go bits of endless chatter, tho' to us it
    matters not.
"Sally Splatter's gotten fatter, like Miss
    Dollop and Miss Slob!
'Tis short distance for a damsel to turn
    into formless blob!"

* * * * * *

gend	gack	sing	-	singe
gile	gope	lung	-	lunge
gub	geb	bing	-	binge
gade	gafe	tinge	-	ting
gyfe	guct	bange	-	bang
grise	gunt	ring	-	ringe
gyt	gerd	swinge	-	swing
gant	garp	spring	-	springe
gult	gime	slung	-	slunge
gex	gess	slinge	-	sling
gud	gire	sting	-	stinge
gisp	gact			
gyde	glap	wage	-	wag
gock	gict	gag	-	gage
giss	gymp	stage	-	stag
gir	gute	huge	-	hug
gurn	ger	rag	-	rage
gluff	gipe	sag	-	sage
gake	glax	luge	-	lug
gyck	gemp	dog	-	doge
glat	gyd	swag	-	swage
gine	gret	mage	-	mag
gug	gabe	cag	-	cage
gelk	goke	loge	-	log

dingy	Virgil	figment
enlarge	disgust	burgess
ginger	tangent	argent
goddess	plunger	gypsum
suggest	submerge	stringent
gymnast	gorget	germane
urgent	gentry	turgite
gesture	grapnel	margent
goblet	infringe	virgate
German	rampage	
guppy	gosling	urgency
clergy	pungent	allergy
fungus	turgid	contingent
gypsy	umbrage	harbinger
gentile	mustang	engender
margin	expunge	indulgent
magnet	stingy	messenger
engage	gulden	astringent
gender	converge	subterfuge
giblets	ignite	porringer
gallon	ginseng	insurgent
congest	ingest	passenger
enrage	largess	effulgence
gibbet	turgent	indulgence
gullet	impinge	contingency

badge	barge	wage
budge	bulge	huge
wedge	plunge	stage
fudge	indulge	rampage
bridge	submerge	oblige

bag	–	badge	hinge	urge
rig		ridge	dirge	fadge
bug		budge	age	midge
judge		jug	edge	barge
ledge		leg	bilge	surge
brig		bridge	twinge	Norge
lodge		log	flange	cringe
fidge		fig	swedge	skedge
smug		smudge	marge	gorge
Madge		mag	plunge	sedge
slug		sludge	page	splurge
pudge		pug	pledge	plodge
kedge		keg	large	merge
dreg		dredge	hedge	tedge
dodge		dog	verge	scrunge
crag		cradge	nudge	serge
snug		snudge	fledge	podge
gadge		gag	purge	trudge
drug		drudge	forge	Hodge

In multisyllable words, final unaccented <u>age</u> = (ĭj). It may be part of a baseword or it may be a suffix referring to a relationship with.

Spelling aid: Final unaccented (ĭj) in multisyllable words = <u>age</u>.

bandage	luggage	package
baggage	tankage	ventage
corkage	raftage	vintage
cribbage	pondage	vantage
draftage	cartage	graftage
pottage	cordage	carnage
bondage	grillage	pillage
crimpage	meltage	
ambage	suffrage	parsonage
mintage	standage	pastorage
wardage	windage	plunderage
pontage	ullage	appendage
truckage	scrummage	assemblage
stumpage	siltage	personage

sh

ship	cash	share	wash
shot	crush	shank	squash
shun	shirt	shape	shrunk
shy	shire	shelve	shrove
ash	sled	splash	shroff
blush	flesh	slosh	shin
shack	mash	shog	flash
hash	marsh	shunt	hush
rush	short	shan't	pash
shad	shote	dash	shrank
shade	shive	flush	shrike
trash	shod	plash	shrift
sham	swish	pash	shrive
shame	shrug	shush	shend
smash	shut	shave	rash
slush	shred	shelf	shock
fish	shag	slash	shrill
mesh	sash	tush	shrink
shaft	shalt	harsh	shrine
shake	shift	gash	fash
shrimp	sharp	plush	shark
shell	shine	shim	shrub
shore	shirk	shop	shuck
brash	clash	shorn	shale
brush	dish	Welsh	mush

brandish	shellac	accomplish
dervish	skittish	embellish
shaddock	sheldrake	establish
rubbish	blandish	shadberry
shamrock	cashmere	shilly-shally
sunshine	enshrine	Suffix -ish:
shellfish	shallop	selfish
publish	shoddy	sixish
vanquish	shallot	girlish
English	shindig	impish
kingfish	burnish	pinkish
shilling	Oshkosh	sickish
shutter	furbish	warmish
shipshape	skirmish	dampish
shimmer	shammer	Turkish
sherry	shanty	waspish
sherbet	tarnish	Suffix -ship:
shelty	Yiddish	clerkship
grogshop	shrapnel	lordship
marshal	shudder	kingship
droshky	shippon	hardship
worship	shindy	wardship
shatter	shimmy	partnership
shammy	varnish	censorship

<u>ch</u> (ch)

chin	pinch	crunch	chare
chest	punch	clinch	chark
chock	chump	charm	chine
choke	chug	finch	chink
bench	chop	starch	larch
arch	chant	champ	lynch
churn	branch	drench	niche
chore	chase	chafe	chirr
chick	chuff	mulch	chirk
chat	chirp	chart	stench
parch	chuck	torch	smirch
inch	chip	chime	chirm
chess	chap	flinch	churl
ranch	chape	lurch	scrinch
trench	blanch	chard	glunch
chum	brunch	chinch	grinch
church	check	filch	munch
chaff	charge	scorch	cinch
chance	chose	wench	hanch
birch	chunk	winch	squelch
belch	lunch	quench	much
char	gulch	chide	such
chill	hunch	churr	chit
perch	chive	trunch	curch
march	rich	blench	conch

chastise	archer	Chibchan
chattel	archduke	chervil
checkmate	chancel	chessel
Cheddar	chapman	cheddite
chubby	trenchant	Chartism
enchant	poncho	chaplet
urchin	franchise	charnel
orchard	chitchat	chantry
hunchback	ostrich	charlock
enrich	chitter	champac
parchment	chirrup	chatter
channel	chandler	chanty
chapter	challis	pyxchest
charter	chaffinch	
cherry	entrench	enchantress
chigger	surcharge	chancellor
chipmunk	chuddar	champerty
henchman	discharge	chatterbox
merchant	planchet	Childermas
sandwich	chaffer	Chippendale
chestnut	chamfron	merchandise
attach	charry	muttonchop
challenge	penchant	wanchancy
Chester	chukker	checkerberry
chapstick	chamfer	unflinchingly

ch (k) ch (sh)

chi	Christy	chef
cham	paschal	chic
Tech	bacchic	chute
chord	Bacchus	schwa
Pasch	Lychnis	chaps
hecht	chalcid	cache
chasm	cichlid	hilch
chyle	diptych	borsch
scheme	technics	Schick
chrome	chordate	creche
chrism	chondrus	schorl
chlore	triptych	Porsche
	cromlech	
Chris	Canchrus	chiffon
orchid	chladnite	chassis
anchor	splanchnic	Schwinn
archil	strychnine	chevron
archon		mustache
tulchan	orchestral	pinscher
archive	chlorpicrin	boschbok

Chords on the organ,
Creche actors convene,
Chiffon on pine garlands –
The Christmas scene!

123

When is final (ch) spelled <u>tch</u>?

	crunch	crutch
	parch	patch
	march	match
	pinch	pitch
witch	twitch	catchup
etch	watch	Satchmo
itch	hatch	hatchet
latch	blotch	kitchen
notch	stitch	pitcher
Scotch	smutch	ratchet
snatch	stetch	satchel
switch	fletch	Mitchell
ditch	quitch	hatchment
botch	vetch	stitchwort
catch	cratch	patchwork
clutch	stretch	hatchel
batch	hitch	stretcher
crotch	ketch	watchword
fetch	scutch	dispatch
hutch	scratch	futchel
sketch	fitch	crosshatch
hotch	ratch	Gretchen
Dutch	swatch	Natchez

<u>th</u> (th)

thin	twelfth	width
thank	moth	forth
theme	thrips	froth
theft	thir	firth
bath	thole	math
mirth	Thor	depth
sixth	thwart	cloth
filth	thwack	tenth
thane	thyrse	throng
Smith	thig	thrift
thing	thill	thirst
worth	spilth	thrice
third	Goth	thrum
thud	birth	thrash
north	throb	thresh
broth	strengthen	thrush
throne	berth	thirl
thrill	thrive	thorp
thrust	thorn	thrave
think	myth	throve
thick	troth	thug
pith	path	
thong	thump	anthem
fifth	girth	athlete
length	lath	Arthur

125

panther	forthwith	norther
anther	lengthwise	swarthy
hundredth	strengthen	murther
thirty		further
thermos	aftermath	brethren
Sabbath	thunderstone	farthing
ethnic		northern
anthrax	th (th)	furthest
canthus		farthest
enthuse	the	farthingale
Carthage	thy	furthermore
bismuth	this	withstanding
filthy	than	
mammoth	that	
thermal	them	(th) (th)
thunder	thus	bath – bathe
Kenneth	then	cloth clothe
Kathryn	these	lath lathe
menthol	those	lith lithe
thallus	thine	scath scathe
thrombin	thence	swath swathe
birthplace		snath snathe
blacksmith	worthy	tithe
enthrone	farther	scythe
		blithe

wh (hw)

wish – whish	whence – wince	Whig –wig
wine whine	wile while	wise why's
when wen	whale wale	whin win
welp whelp	whack WAC	why Y
whet wet	witch which	watt what
wist whist	welt whelt	wap whap
whit wit	whacks wax	wort whort

* *

wilk – whilk	wheg - weg
whift wift	weff wheff
wheck weck	wilp whilp
wiss whiss	wamp whamp

---

whang	erstwhile	winchat
whelk	whimper	whipstitch
whid	whiffler	whetstone
whim	whippet	whitter
whip	wherry	whiz-bang
whirl	whiffet	Whitsun
whist	whimsy	whipstock
whiz	whitrack	whipcord
whir	whisper	whapping
white	whisky	whopping
whelm	whinstone	whapper

whop	whimbrel	whopper
whiff	whinny	wharfinger
whorl	whiplash	Whitsuntide
whisker	whirlwind	whippersnapper

where
there
to
do
of

The Whether Man

On Channel 2 from 2:00 to 3:00 on Sat. is the best TV! It's the wise and witty Whether Man. He cares a whit for a lot of things. In just five sittings I have gotten this "info":

Why lads tend to yell and girls to whisper,
Why we get a whiplash in a car crash,
Why we wet a whetstone to sharpen stuff,
Why we mix *y*'s and *h*'s.

What watt bulb to use in what lamp,
What welts, wens, warts and cysts are,
What whelps do while the fox and the vixen are
    in the den,
What the fastest time is for a whippet dog in a
    race.

<u>Where</u> we can spot will-o-the wisp,
<u>Where</u> there are horses with no whinny,
<u>Where</u> we get the term whippersnapper,
<u>Where</u> the biggest whales can be spotted.

<u>Which</u> is the wickĕd witch in the "Wizard of
    Oz,"
<u>Which</u> ancestors wore wigs or whiskers,
<u>Which</u> sort of whiffs can kill us,
<u>Which</u> whish in the car is a signal to stop
    quickly.

The Whether Man has discussed the
manner we can tell:

<u>whether</u> whacks are the best method of ending
    whines and whispers,
<u>whether</u> a wet or a dry brush is best to whisk
    off a wisp of web,
<u>whether</u> to get flat or to run if a whirlwind is
    going to whiz by,
                    AND
<u>whether</u> or not a lad is telling a whopper!

phone	orphan	morphene
phi	Philco	phosgene
Phil	dolphin	phyllode
phot	Memphis	sulphite
graph	phantom	phantasm
Ralph	sulphur	samphire
phlox	camphor	phyllome
nymph	phrensy	phosphite
phase	philter	blaspheme
lymph	Phyllis	sphagnum
humph	camphol	sphygmic
sylph	telpher	sphincter
sphinx	Phillips	phosphide
sphere	pamphlet	triphthong
phrase	phosphor	
sphene	diphthong	Alphonso
klepht	phosphate	atmosphere

The Whopper

There is a big sandwich named Whopper
That is quite a hunger-stopper –
A glutton's rare prize,
Just mammoth in size,
With catchup and chips as a topper!

Pronounce nonsense words. You will recognize a real word. Use it <u>orally</u> in a sentence.

* *

golph	phycks
wysh	micks
whyle	phynch
buph	whyph
swysh	phancy
phelt	phlag
drypht	phlyp
bluph	phrysky
phyne	sufphicks
thrypht	snyph
chyme	sufpher
shyp	clyph
whysker	elph
twelphth	wytch
gruph	rydge

Words ending in sibilant sounds regularly spell their plurals with <u>es</u>. The suffix adds a syllable to the word.

<u>S</u>	<u>X</u>	<u>Z</u>
presses	axes	fuzzes
misses	taxes	jazzes
lasses	boxes	buzzes
messes	lynxes	fizzes
classes	fixes	blitzes
hisses	waxes	whizzes
masses	foxes	adzes

<u>ch</u>	<u>sh</u>
crutches	dashes
matches	marshes
witches	wishes
torches	splashes
itches	dishes
hunches	brushes
pinches	clashes

An extra syllable is also pronounced when <u>s</u> is added to words with a final sibilant sound, plus <u>e</u>.

<u>ce</u>	<u>ge</u>	<u>se</u>, <u>ze</u>
dances	stages	horses
laces	fringes	roses
ices	badges	uses
fences	cages	lapses
braces	hedges	senses

132

Suffix <u>es</u>:

Jim sloshes a lot when he washes the puppy.
He splashes himself and gets wet as a guppy.

The stately sultan simply hates clashes
And utters an order, "Apply <u>sixty</u> lashes!"

Elvis Dar switches his nines and his sixes.
He mixes his numbers and gets into fixes!

Sam's a sportsman with lots of hats.
He golfs and sprints and punts and bats.

The Shortstop gets hits in, and pitches and
    catches.
While Third Base gets bitten, and itches and
    scratches!

If a man ignores signals, takes chances and
    dashes,
That jester can bet on the grimmest of crashes.

The bird perches pertly for quite a long term,
But then lurches curtly and lunches on worm!

I didn't complete that tome for ages–
It had six hundred and fifty pages!

Sam hitches his britches on red 'lastic braces.
He pops these suspenders, expanding his chest.
So sister Marce flashes her smile that is silver,
And pops rubber bands from HER braces in
    jest!

I try to be careful – my bike's kept by latches,
With locks on its spokes – but still a man
    snatches!

My grandad is ninety and tends to his roses,
And rocks in his rocker and catnaps and dozes.

PLUMP POLLY

O, this is a tale that is hard to tell
Of plump Polly Merrick – she stuffs till
    unwell.
She crunches on crackers and splurges on
    cakes,
Indulges in bonbons and gorges on shakes.

Her dresses sport bulges – her mirror's no use.
Her frame still enlarges – she makes no excuse.
She flinches at inches and stitches, unstopping.
But then munches rich desserts dolloped with
    topping!

It's sad that this lumpy lass can not express
The thing that's a problem, that makes such
    distress.
For if she gets bigger, this plump Polly Merrick
Will end up in a coffin – to be lifted by
    derrick!

LONG-CHANCE CHAD

Long-Chance Chad is quite a bettor.
Quite a braggart and go-getter.
To the races go he MUST –
Likes the faces, likes the dust.
Works on hunches, trusts to luck.
Stands in line to bet his buck.
Fetches tickets on fastest stepper.
Quenches his thirst with a Dr. Pepper.
Places himself at the starting gate,
Braces himself and converses with Fate.

He judges despondently, curses the clock,
Bumps into fence's pole, drenches a sock,
Twitches and glances and winces and etches
A picture of losses in last of the stretches!
Chastises himself for attendance here,
Rises from doldrums when bells interfere.
The pack rushes past and he thinks, "Was I
    wise?"
He surges to senses and has a surprise:
"The long shot dubbed Ack-Ack is first!"
        He's a winner!
Chad collects on his stubs and totes riches
    to dinner!

SPOT THE ODD

Read each line and decide which word is unlike the others in meaning.

1. lasses   <u>crosses</u>   misses   girls
2. kisses   pecks   perches   hugs
3. fixes   fives   sixes   nines
4. remnants   watches   swatches   patches
5. flashes   signals   sashes   flags
6. crashes   smashes   stitches   clashes
7. lashes   itches   noses   hips
8. trunks   latches   clamps   locks
9. snatches   switches   filches   robs
10. lunches   lurches   dinners   snacks
11. pitches   slashes   catches   bats
12. scratches   mashes   rashes   itches
13. stretches   enlarges   charges   swells
14. passes   surprises   runs   punts

SPOT THE ODD

Read each line and decide which word is unlike the others in meaning.

1. chomps   <u>chastises</u>   munches   crunches

2. roses   or<u>ch</u>ids   asters   places

3. ages   indulges   spends   splurges

4. curses   drenches   sloshes   splashes

5. tells   glimpses   chats   converses

6. dozes   catnaps   braces   slumbers

7. winces   twitches   judges   flinches

8. etches   sketches   sculpts   quenches

9. inches   dances   yards   furlongs

10. rushes   pages   surges   rises

11. races   matches   contests   riches

12. belts   shirts   hunches   dresses

13. graces   fetches   gets   collects

14. fills   losses   gorges   stuffs

<u>Preparation:</u> Review:– auditory recognition of syl. and accent. (Level I Preparation)

– (ū) after <u>l</u>, <u>r</u>, <u>s</u> = (o͞o) (Level II)

– <u>r</u>-controlled vowels (when <u>r</u> falls at the end of word or when it is followed by any consonant except another <u>r</u>. V<u>r</u> words follow syl. division rules)

<u>Explanation:</u> Level V may be presented before or with Level IV. Present each formula individually with much drill in application. As Formula I is presented, the student should learn to chant line 1 (below), and line 2 with Formula 2, etc.

Concepts to Develop

When one con. stands between two vowels, the syls. may divide before or after the con., depending on the first vowel sound.

Student marks vowels and con., beginning with first vowel in word <u>o p e n</u>

                                               v c v

Page	Formulas:	Chant	Example
140	1. V´/CV	1. A vowel at the end of an unaccented syl. is long	ō´pen
141	2. VC´/V	2. A vowel in a closed syl. is short	rŏb´in
	3. V/CV´	3. At the end of an unaccented syl.,	
		e, o, and u are half-long ĕ/lect´ ŏ/mit´	ů/nite´
		i and vowel y are short	dĭ/vide´
		a is obscure (a̍) or (ŭ)	ca̍/nal´

For Reading: Applying formulas to two-syl. words*

Applying formulas to three-syl. words which combine VCV and VCCV

For Spelling: (It is important that the student learn to pronounce spelling words in syllables and to spell each syl. as a unit. <u>pa´per</u>, NOT <u>pap´er</u>
VC´V words are irregular for spelling. Rabbit words are more common than ro<u>b</u>in words. See Level I.

1. A long vowel sound at the end of a medial syl. is spelled with a single vowel. <u>ō´pen</u>
2. (ŭ) in a closed syl. must be spelled <u>u</u>. <u>cul´prit</u>
   (ŭ) in an accented syl. must be spelled <u>u</u>. <u>but´ton</u>
3. (ŭ) at the end of an unaccented syl. must be spelled <u>a</u>. <u>ba ton´</u>
   <u>ma ture´</u> – <u>mut´ter</u>   <u>sa lon´</u> – <u>sul´len</u>   <u>ca nal´</u> – <u>cun´ning</u>
          <u>ga lash´</u> – <u>gul´ly</u>   <u>ca det´</u> – <u>cud´dy</u>
   Exceptions sometimes caused by Latin prefixes <u>suc</u>, <u>suf</u>, <u>sup</u>. <u>succumb</u>, <u>suffice</u>, <u>supply</u>, etc. are irregular for spelling.
4. (s) = <u>c</u> after a vowel if followed by <u>e</u>, <u>i</u>, or <u>y</u>. <u>ice</u> <u>precinct</u>

Dividing V<u>CC</u>V words with a con. digraph which sticks together in a syl. and behaves as single con. Apply VCV formulas: go´<u>ph</u>er, bo<u>th</u>´er, a <u>sh</u>ore´

Dividing VCCV words with a con. blend which behaves as a single con. <u>A´pril</u>

*Student reads unfamiliar words three possible ways and is told which is correct.

ī́|ris	cider	raven	vinyl
open	apex	story	baby
bison	duty	student	cadent
humid	cedar	stupid	yogart
Irish	climax	Salem	blazon
label	capon	silent	bicorn
labor	brocade	tyrant	basic
Tyler	crazy	Trojan	Babel
latex	cony	votive	cosine
libel	Cuban	lazy	judo
zero	furor	regent	docent
even	genus	cylix	edict
crocus	gravy	crony	dotard
locate	gyro	feline	Amos
fiber	mason	local	cogent
decent	lotus	thesis	cubit
lucid	legal	super	credo
final	Jacob	vapor	dative
future	pupil	chorus	doby
motive	precinct	favor	femur
basin	julep	razor	dotage
Roman	idol	tiger	latent
Egypt	fury	forum	Adolph
oval	hero	vacant	hogan
demon	holy	locust	omen

V̆C´V

ăt|om	Briton	liver	shiver
cabin	Robert	baron	novel
figure	azure	gavel	prison
comic	vigor	lyric	presence
credit	valor	lozenge	bigot
logic	lizard	chronic	tremor
critic	polish	rapid	snivel
volume	ravish	Philip	tacit
vivid	placid	patent	vizard
damage	Danube	ravel	wizard
clamor	gratis	savage	vigil
modern	colic	river	sliver
decade	satire	bevel	Spanish
tragic	physics	adage	trivet
parish	polyp	chevy	vary
legend	seven	legume	tepid
panel	shrivel	globule	visage
denim	rivet	garish	talon
panic	satin	placard	stipule
peril	rosin	livid	felon
gerund	tenure	penance	spirit
radish	frigid	Saturn	spigot
project	lavish	seraph	tenant
Carol	cherub	static	valance
relic	coral	timid	tribute

V̄′CV V̆C′V

tŏ|by	pilot	petal	famish
tŏn|ic	prudent	cupid	halo
glamor	totem	major	rigid
chisel	profit	linen	token
Cajun	slogan	menu	image
unit	saber	spider	robot
frugal	pyrex	grocer	blemish
tropics	tripod	cherish	bonus
lunar	spiral	arid	flavor
biceps	merit	British	blazer
process	veto	civic	sinus
ego	vital	crater	Latin
tribune	product	dilate	evil
wager	craven	camel	phonics
Yukon	bevy	meter	rodent
polo	puny	pedal	item
Hazel	rotate	digit	limit
humor	level	epic	rumor
comet	rival	pagan	frolic
Avon	nylon	finish	madam
Midas	planet	facet	tulip
topaz	stylus	tunic	hobo
tyrant	onyx	gyrate	olive
civil	larynx	closet	tavern
tumult	clever	model	culex

VCV

Open and closed syl.   VC/CV + V´/CV

cav´al‖cade	supercede	Oc‖to‖ber
de´‖cen‖cy	Protestant	corrosive
everglade	sepul<u>ch</u>er	component
paraffin	Oberlin	opponent
parallel	monar<u>ch</u>y	adhesive
heronry	cavalry	magneto
demonstrate	devastate	torpedo
regency	potency	Bermuda
desiccate	isinglass	albumen
colonnade	columbine	conducive
potentate	<u>ch</u>ivalry	exclusive
designate	baluster	volcano
poverty	Palestine	inclusive
rivalry	pedestal	mandamus
novelty	sinister	lumbago
reconcile	vacillate	tornado

At the end of unaccented syl., e̠, o̠, and u̠ are half-long.

(e̊)	(o̊)	(ů) (o͞o)
pre̊∣tend´	bro̊∣cade´	Lů∣zon´
defend	rotund	superb
before	romance	usurp
serene	propose	unite
belong	protect	Lucerne
beside	opine	humane
depend	morose	brunet
event	procure	Sudan
refer	obese	ukase
select	provide	crusade
recite	cohere	
prepare	provoke	jujitsu
remote	produce	

Memo to the Major:

Select. Prepare. Unite! Defend!
(Then act humanely at the end!)

VCV

bū|tane	promote	epo<u>ch</u>
mĕt|al	module	brunet
bė|gun´	edit	cremate
robin	Venus	moral
desire	sheriff	vomit
human	very	decide
modest	lever	molest
moment	opal	curate
recent	deduct	perish
Roger	medal	humus
suburb	pony	propel
motor	refuse	reduce
prevent	heron	Helen
lemon	recess	sonar
colon	secure	grenade
presence	tenor	Judy
elope	debate	Lucerne
fever	vacate	s<u>ch</u>olar
<u>ch</u>emist	<u>ch</u>ronic	punish
herald	tutor	florist
music	frolic	elapse
erase	tumor	quiver
Poland	device	proverb
never	Rover	borax

seg´|re|gate	calculate	syn<u>ch</u>ronize
porcupine	diplomat	piccolo
absolute	suffocate	reprobate
balcony	singular	succulent
compromise	octopus	syncopate
persecute	insulin	turbojet
insulate	antelope	surrogate
improvise	congregate	exodus
amputate	factory	anchovy
acrobat	competent	obsolete
incubate	Anthony	synthesize
symphony	abdomen	correlate
ambulance	corrugate	macrocosm
execute	postulate	phosphorus
arsenic	succotash	abrogate
alcohol	pendulum	accolade
innocent	pantomime	arsenal
mercury	luxury	Bethlehem
daffodil	instrument	communism
circulate	envelope	rectory
complement	formulate	subjugate
advocate	persecute	supplement
hypnotize	mandolin	turbulent
arrogant	symbolize	victory

V/CV´

ĭ/CV´

Pronounce three ways:

tiny:

tī´/nў	lily	July
tĭn´/ў	pity	rely
tĭ/nў´	chili	defy
		deny

V/CV´	V/CV + VC/CV	
dĭ|vide´	dĭ|rec´|tor	barricade
divine	pimento	complicate
cigar	synopsis	continent
divorce	divergence	difficult
divulge	Britannic	cultivate
digest	sirocco	confident
dilute	philander	Eskimo
brigade	hidalgo	estimate
direct	directly	indicate
Tibet	viburnum	maximum
shikar	stiletto	negligent
Brinell	synoptic	multitude
quinone	divulgate	sacrifice
bricole	VC´/CV + V/CV	reprimand
diwan	can´|nĭ|bal	syndicate
cymar	accident	vestibule
gisarne	altitude	aspirin
sitar	antidote	terminate
chicane	applicant	pertinent

VCV

sen´|sĭ|tive	ventilate	amplitude
varsity	supplicate	centrifuge
institute	servitude	larriken
magnitude	principal	vertigo
captivate	mannikin	massicot
candidate	intimate	pemmican
centipede	fabricate	Anglican
compliment	cardigan	larvicide
dignity	condiment	subsidize
hurricane	optimist	detriment
irritate	obligate	oxidize
fascinate	milliner	Merrimac
practical	officer	effigy
sentiment	ordinance	entity
substitute	palpitate	circinate
terminal	pestilence	exigence
vertical	surgical	Biblicist
pessimist	extricate	classicize
longitude	quantity	mysticism
furniture	sentinel	pessimism
culminate	subsidy	skepticism
admiral	lexicon	optimism
artifact	occident	whirligig
cardinal	continence	pesticide

VCCV
VC/Cȧ

When the word a is unaccented in a sentence, how is it pronounced?
         - - - Here's a pencil.   (ŭ)
         - - - It's a dog.   (ŭ)
At the end of an unaccented syllable, what is the sound of a?

com′mȧ	vodka	momma
stanza	Vesta	Hella
Anna	Scylla	bregma
extra	Emma	con<u>ch</u>a
delta	Kenya	chacma
yucca	calla	pinna
larva	olla	Belma
tundra	henna	chibcha
canna	naphtha	poppa
Edna	Bella	hubba-hubba
Inca	circa	Martha
gamma	dicta	
villa	salta	chin|chir̆|lȧ
vista	lemma	Atlanta
stigma	britska	umbrella
plasma	cella	Calcutta
junta	gemma	alfalfa
magma	colza	antenna
dogma	Volga	scintilla
ultra	Orsha	vendetta
alpha	Donna	mammilla

à‖like´	apart	ago	cravat
abide	arose	acute	cajole
abode	atone	averse	cavort
adapt	aloft	abuse	galore
afire	agog	adore	lament
ajar	avenge	alive	galosh
alack	alarm	arise	canard
amid	avert	cadet	capote
amaze	amidst	salute	casern
adorn	awoke	lapel	<u>ch</u>arade
aline	aside	along	manure

The sounds of <u>a</u>: at the end of an accented syllable - - - ā´/CV
in a closed syllable - - - - - - - - - - - ăC´/V
at the end of unaccented syl. - - - - - - à/CV´

pā‖per	canal	manage	adopt
văn‖ish	amuse	cadence	tariff
à‖lone´	flavor	alert	canine
Mabel	valid	kapok	balance
Japan	razor	cavern	Clarence
basis	aware	caper	amend
Brazil	travel	baton	native
hazard	vacate	gravel	caress
awake	navy	mature	Adam
banish	salon	damage	David

150

V/CV + VC/CV		VC´/CV + V/CV
Ȧ|las´|kȧ	stalactite	cin´|nȧ|mon
Apollo	stalagmite	pentagon
vanilla	<u>ch</u>arisma	buffalo
majestic	amalgam	terrapin
abundant	statistics	escapade
amendment	apartment	emphasize
maternal	canasta	Texaco
asunder	marimba	narrative
agenda	patella	ornament
cadenza	avellan	octagon
bacillus	calyptra	signature
alumna	apostate	moccasin
paternal	papilla	marmalade
akimbo	magenta	invalid
Aladdin	galactose	pharmacy
catalpa	Camorra	excavate
calypso	flabellum	Singapore
abandon	cavetto	aggravate
malignant	canescent	alphabet
Damascus	Tarentum	hexagon
Jakarta	thalassic	escalade
savanna	sphragistic	Calgary
placenta	<u>Ch</u>arybdis	sacrament
fraternal	Magellan	ostracize
malinger	cavalla	summarize

Pronounce these nonsense syllables three ways.
(a is never accented at the end of a word.)

* *

pita

pī′tȧ   prily   grida

pĭt′ȧ   futa   clapo

pĭ tā′   tody   slica

furo	demo	skepa
sena	prima	fyna
muta	pocy	struda
hity	goca	queno
dada	phota	slasy
moda	risa	elo
tefa	bady	upy
sono	vida	ito
pify	drago	eka
haka	brosy	smyda
tiba	sleta	eso
nila	trano	uva
cipy	tify	opa
vado	typo	imy

152

Jumbled Words

Read the nonsense word as it is.
Then unscramble the syllables to form real words.

a graph păr´

no ca´ vol

pe´ tôr do

bal´ ny co

bate in´ cu

pha al´ bet

ment ôr´ na

lo pol´ A

ci dent ac´

phone ta dic´

an´ lope te

to vic´ ry

stru in´ ment

na dan´ ban

the´ ca dral

ry a sal´

rate sep´ a

ly It´ a

thy sym´ pa

ma´ to to

ty van´ i

ta vi´ min

dy o mel´

ti con´ nent

nan´ ba a

na ten´ an

lo dip´ mat

su´ man pẽr

ta pen´ gon

corn ni u´

u´ verse ni

pli com´ ment

VCCV

A consonant digraph sticks together and acts as a single consonant.

V´/ C V	V C´/ V	V / C V´
mo <u>ch</u>a	**e<u>ch</u> o**	**a <u>sh</u>ore**

trī´|<u>th</u>ing	clo<u>th</u>ing	cel´|lŏ|phane
ether	gopher	atrophy
typhus	usher	sympathy
sca<u>th</u>ing	bo<u>th</u>er	artichoke
ethos	hyphen	harpsi<u>ch</u>ord
cipher	ashore	dictaphone
o<u>ch</u>er	whe<u>th</u>er	saxophone
lethal	python	empathy
	method	Ne<u>th</u>erlands
sli<u>th</u>´|er	e<u>ch</u>o	sophistry
methane	Rachel	Be|thes´|da
pithy	Athens	catharsis
cathode	duchess	lethargic
Gothic	fa<u>th</u>om	cartography
bethel	siphon	
zephyr	wither	
tether	Ethel	
ethics	bro<u>ch</u>ure	
zither	aphid	
<u>thi</u><u>th</u>er	ra<u>th</u>er	
	bishop	
rĕ|shape´	kosher	

VCCV
(consonant blends)

When two consonants stand between vowels, syllable division usually occurs between the two consonants. Occasionally, the two consonants form a blend which sticks together and functions as one consonant.

Pronounce the word, dividing between the two consonants. If a word is not recognized, treat the two consonants as a blend which sticks together and use VCV formulas.

Example: regret

| 1. reg´ ret | 2. re´gret (V´CV) |
| reg ret´ | re gret´ (V CV´) |

v|ccv	VC/CV or VCcv		
mā´|cron	fab|ric	sacred	drastic
replace	di|graph	escape	begrudge
protrude	program	okra	suspence
protract	migrate	cyclone	neglect
hybred	prosper	reflect	deplore
microbe	hatred	pistol	dacron
betwixt	depress	escort	vibrate
patron	copra	zebra	duplex
Cyprus	mascot	costume	pester
hydrant	secrete	cypress	nitrate
April	discuss	fragrant	vagrant
declare	trespass	citrus	despise
abrupt	putrid	Chrysler	rascal
refresh	public	restore	cobra
oblige	suspect	secret	sublime
recluse	tablet	respond	agree
between	eclipse	decline	flagrant

<u>s</u> and <u>c</u> Between Vowels

Pronounce each word two ways, using the two sounds of <u>s</u> (s) (z)

close	adverb	verb
use	noun	verb
excuse	noun	verb
abuse	noun	verb

<u>s</u> between two vowels is more often pronounced (z).
(s) after a vowel and followed by <u>e</u>, <u>i</u>, <u>y</u> is regularly spelled <u>c</u>.

rice	rise	recess	resist
face	phase	conduce	confuse
twice	wise	precinct	present
device	devise	entice	comprise
advice	advise	induce	infuse
recent	resent	suffice	surprise
spice	despise	precedent	president
mice	demise	vice	revise
fleece	cheese	decide	reside

Wise mice this device quite despise.
(It saves spices and brings quick demise!)

Seventh Grade Rally

"O.K., class, let's get on! Line up by your first name. If it has two syl., splits like the word <u>hu´man</u>, and is accented on the first syl., line up here."

"Ho, ho, ho! It's a line-up, just like a precinct!"

"But she thinks we're human!"

"Let's name you The Demons. O.K., Demons!
Amy, Hiram, Mason, Moses,
Judy, Cyrus, Steven, Otis,
Cecil, Lucy, Leland, Hubert,
David, Nigel, Ruby, Lotus!"

"Fine and dandy! If your name has two syl., splits like the word <u>sec´ond</u>, and is accented on the first syl., line up THERE.

"Yi, yi, yi! You're second best!"

"Nope, that's not so, we're just like LINE #2."

"You're correct! You're Devils too!
Karen, Gerard, Gretel, Clarence,
Gary, Gladys, Gavin, Florence,
Adam, Robin, Sybil, Carol,
Helen, Trevor, Philip, Lorenz!"

"So why is part of the gang left? Will you
get in line as I asked when I name you?
Get a crony, step in silence,
    Yell in cadence at the Pep.
    Lyman, Felix, Opal, Peter,
    Efram, Hazel, let's get hep!"

"What's with the rest of us who are left?"

"No more static! Get more rapid,
Seven denimed Devils, SO
Alex, Gavin, Robert, Basil,
Colin, Eric, Roger, go!"

"T.G.I.F.! You're too much!"

VCV

An Eskimo's difficult life
Has minimal marital strife.
This adapted landlubber
Digests his whale blubber,
Then merrily noses his wife!

"You're obesity's caused me remorse.
You're rotund and revolting, Miss Norse!
Prepare to reduce, or
I'll quit as producer!"
The actress, agape, said, "Of course!"

A hip adolescent named Kevin
Watched T.V. 'til eleven.
He felt rather lanky,
His mind was a blanky
When awakened by parents at seven.

Synonyms are <u>gaze</u> and <u>stare</u>.
Antonyms are <u>here</u> and <u>there</u>.
Homonyms are <u>pear</u> and <u>pair</u>.
I must remember them. Beware!

Vowel digraphs

Dipthongs = vowel blends that behave as digraphs (one sound) in words. <u>ou</u>, <u>ow</u>, <u>oi</u>, <u>oy</u>

<u>Syl. Division</u>: Digraphs and dipthongs are assigned a sound which is unchanged in open and closed syl. <u>raisin</u> When digraphs and dipthongs occur at the syl. division line, they present fewer problems than does a single vowel.

Regular Spelling for Long Vowel Sounds:

at end of syl.	in final closed syl.	at end of word
<u>a</u>	<u>a</u> - <u>e</u>*	<u>ay</u>
<u>e</u>	<u>ee</u> (1-syl. word)	
	<u>e</u> - <u>e</u> (multi-syl. word) <u>ee</u>	
<u>i</u>	<u>i</u> - <u>e</u>	<u>y</u>
<u>o</u>	<u>o</u> - <u>e</u>	<u>ow</u>
<u>u</u>	<u>u</u> - <u>e</u>	<u>ue</u>

Situation spelling pages in Workbook require student to consider where long vowel occurs:
1. At end of syl, use single letter; <u>a</u>, <u>e</u>, <u>i</u>, <u>o</u>, <u>u</u>.
2. Before one final con. sound, use <u>a-e</u>, <u>e-e</u>, <u>i-e</u>, <u>o-e</u>, <u>u-e</u>.
   EXCEPTION: (ē) in 1-syl. word = <u>ee</u> (f<u>ee</u>t)
3. Final in a word, use <u>ay</u>, <u>ee</u>, <u>y</u>, <u>ow</u> and <u>ue</u>.

<u>Page</u>	<u>Reading</u>	<u>Spelling</u>
162	ee (ē)	Irregular in multi-syl. words
165	ea (ē) (ĕ) (ā)	Irregular
168	oo (o͞o) (o͝o)	Regular in all situations
172	ai (ā)	Irregular
174	ay (ā)	Regular final situation
176	oa (ō)	Irregular
178	oe (ō)	Irregular
		Learned Word: <u>does</u>
178	ou (ou) (o͞o)	<u>ou</u> (ou) regular in initial and medial situation.
		(<u>ou</u>) (o͞o) irregular for spelling.
181	ow (ou) (ō)	<u>ow</u> (ou) regular in final situation and before vowels
		c<u>ow</u> t<u>ow</u>el
		<u>ow</u> (ō) regular in final situation

*a - e = Vowel-consonant-<u>e</u>

<u>Page</u>	<u>Reading</u>	<u>Spelling</u> (Cont'd.)			
184	au (au)	Regular Spelling:	Initial	Medial	Final
186		(ou) =	ou	ou	ow
189		(au) =	au	au**	aw
191		(oi) =	oi	oi	oy

**EXCEPTION: <u>al</u> – in one-syl. b.w.

194	ue (ū)	Regular in final situation
	Note:	The remaining digraphs are irregular for spelling.
195	ie (ē) (ī)	Irregular for spelling
199	ei (ē) (ā)	Irregular for spelling
200	ey (ē)	Irregular for spelling
201	eu (ū)	Irregular for spelling
202	ew (ū)	Irregular for spelling
207	ui (o͞o)	Irregular for spelling (<u>ui</u> is not a common digraph but it should be recognized before V/V syl. division)
207	ey (ā)	Irregular for spelling

Spelling final (ch) after vowel digraph = <u>ch</u>
final (k) after vowel digraph = <u>k</u>
final (j) after vowel digraph = <u>ge</u>
final (f) (l) after vowel digraph = one <u>f</u>
= one <u>l</u>

208   ous (ŭs)   Suffix and ending

A suffix may be added to a base word ending in a con. after two vowels without changing the spelling of a base word.   <u>boiling</u>   <u>tooted</u>

Suffixes can be added to words ending in a vowel digraph (except <u>ue</u>, <u>ie</u>, <u>oe</u>) without changing the spelling of the base word.
   <u>freeing</u>   <u>snowy</u>   <u>shampooed</u>   <u>sawing</u>

ee (ē)   **3**

feet	cheer	breek
deer	creek	geese
green	deem	geest
jeep	fleece	heeze
meek	greet	leer
peel	heed	screech
queen	jeer	sneesh
screen	keel	steed
seek	leech	squeeze
sheep	teeth	steer
sheer	tee<u>th</u>e	sweer
sleeve	reef	tweed
speech	seep	wheeze
street	sheen	veer
week	skeet	breech
sheet	sleet	
beech	sneer	peep – pep
cheep	spleen	speed sped
greed	leek	beet bet
cheese	beer	bled bleed
deed	breeze	fed feed
eel	creed	steep step
fleet	freeze	met meet
peeve	preen	teen ten
reek	queer	reed red

weed	-	wed	three	whangee
peck	-	peek	bee	thuggee
need	-	Ned	see	vestee
wept	-	weep	fee	absentee
sleep	-	slept	tee	addressee
keep	-	kept	spree	committee
feel	-	fell	flee	chimpanzee
swept	-	sweep	gee	Tennessee
heel	-	hell	glee	
creep	-	crept	wee	canteen
bred	-	breed	tree	esteem
teel	-	tell	Cree	fifteen
feet	-	fet	free	geezer
cheek	-	check	lee	genteel
sen	-	seen	whee	leery
leet	-	let	zee	tweeter
ween	-	wen	bree	sweepstake
Sed	-	seed		tweezers
Stell	-	steel	coffee	sweeny
speel	-	spell	grandee	indeed
beek	-	beck	Parsee	Kathleen
ken	-	keen	mammee	compeer
lees	-	less	pongee	discreet
Seth	-	see<u>the</u>	settee	leeward
wheen	-	when	toffee	Belleek

beeline

beeswax

sixteen

thirteen

weevil

peetweet

beehive

spleenwort

squiglee

VCV

trochee

pewee

tepee

agree

decree

levee

degree

rupee

between

beseech

asleep

sateen

careen

hakeem

career

moreen

redeem

proceed

veneer

shagreen

seventeen

bebeeru

targeteer

carbineer

racketeer

profiteer

buccaneer

volunteer

privateer

chanticleer

muffineer

engineer

mutineer

domineer

shivaree

repartee

refugee

perigee

apogee

referee

pedigree

nominee

jubilee

filigree

divorcee

dungaree

disagree

Cherokee

Keewatin

chickadee

amputee

fricassee

Zebedee

snickersnee

manatee

legatee

ea (ē)

eat	cheap	team	heap
beach	heath	leap	lean
bleat	dean	bleak	peak
beam	beat	mead	neat
ease	leave	fear	peat
cheat	leash	pea	stream
breathe	preach	ream	veal
crease	peal	speak	Lear
bead	squeak	squeal	yeast
bean	scream	teach	wheat
bleach	cease	freak	leaf
creak	lea	cleave	steam
flea	peace	seal	weak
deal	ear	grease	leach
gleam	plead	seat	plea
heave	meal	year	hear
east	gear	weave	steal
cream	meat	zeal	wean
cleat	least	feast	leak
breach	sheaf	pleat	heat
heal	dream	sear	weal
sheath	beast	pleach	bream
sheathe	tweak	tease	neath
lease	please	reap	streak
sneak	each	teal	skean

appeal
beaver
conceal
creature
easel
deacon
increase
feature
peacock
reason
teacup
meantime
weasel
appear
beacon
entreat
Easter
ordeal
peanut
season
seaweed
treaty
eager
easy
heathen

meager
leaflet
seashore
teapot
teamster
treason
sleasy
squeamish
streamer
queasy
impeach
eastern
endear
dreary
congeal
cleaver
bleary
bleachers
beaker
arrear
appease
anneal
seamstress
spearmint
weary

estreat
teasel

underneath
wampumpeag

VCV
bereave
beneath
decrease
bemean
repeat
disease
defeat
repeal
release
bequeath
deceased
retreat
demean
reveal

overhear
disappear
overseas

ea (ĕ)

head	breakfast	VCV
deaf	feather	ahead
bread	weapon	abreast
dealt	heaven	behead
sweat	instead	treachery
thread	heavy	
death	leather	ea (ā)
leapt	meadow	
realm	steady	steak
dread	leaven	great
breast	pleasant	break
cleanse	ready	yea
meant	measure	wear
tread	heather	pear
breath	pheasant	bear
health	weather	swear
stead	sweater	tear
threat	peasant	
dead	zealot	bearing
wealth	pleasure	bugbear
lead	heading	forbearance
spread	headgear	underwear
breadth	endeavor	
read	headquarters	VCV
dreamt	zealotry	overbear

167

oo (o͞o)

moon	boot	tool	scroop
boo	bloom	stoop	shoon
cool	coot	roost	roose
doom	goop	hooch	ooze
food	hoof	booth	cloot
goof	moose	brood	goon
groom	root	croon	Poo
hoot	scoot	loo	shool
loop	snoop	poon	too
mood	stooge	shoo	swoon
noon	smooth	smooch	rood
pool	snoot	spoof	poop
proof	boon	sloop	snook
room	goose	zoom	troop
school	drool	woof	soom
shoot	gloom	oops	snooze
spook	loom	booze	stook
soon	moot	broo	zoo
stool	sooth	coom	whoop
toot	soothe	groove	snool
woo	tooth	loose	poog
boom	coo	snood	goo
roof	broom	swoop	crood
scoop	boost	toom	coon
spoon	choose	noose	Scrooge

oo (o͞o)

shoot	-	shot		chose	-	choose
stop		stoop		noose		nose
swoop		swop		dome		doom
spoke		spook		groove		grove
whoop		whop		rose		roose
snood		snod		bone		boon

hop	-	hoop	-	hope		rote	-	root	-	rot
Lon		loon		lone		coop		cope		cop
mood		mode		mod		Pol		pool		pole
pope		pop		poop		lope		lop		loop
toot		tote		tot		rood		rode		rod
slop		sloop		slope		Tom		toom		tome
con		cone		coon		coot		cote		cot

Oops! A goof!	poop, poop-a-doop
cool igloo	shampoo the goose
lots of goo	a mushroom tattoo
a fool's folly	the hoodlum's booty
a groom's boot	too hot to hoot
Scott scoots	nose in a noose
Ross's rooster	a snooze on the moon
a prof's proof	"Boohoo," sobs Gooch.
as roots rot	It droops and drops buds.
a glob of goop	Poll's pole is in the pool.
a lot of loot	Tote and toot a tot's horn.
a sloppy sloop	a deep groove in the grove

balloon	mushroom	shalloon
goober	bassoon	schooner
hoodlum	booty	footling
igloo	cooly	troostite
bamboo	foolscap	forsooth
rooster	cooncan	galloon
scooter	halloo	skiddoo
sooner	harpoon	raccoon
shampoo	boohoo	karroo
booby	cartoon	
bootleg	dooly	afternoon
pontoon	bloomers	foolhardy
tattoo	oolong	goosander
woozy	gossoon	nincompoop
whoopee	gooly	spoonerism
monsoon	taproot	
moonstone	tarboosh	VCV
festoon	bootee	lagoon
loophole	spontoon	aloof
koodoo	spoony	behoove
lampoon	googly	kazoo
moonwort	Walloon	maroon
buffoon	foolproof	saloon
googol	cooper	dragoon
tomfool	footy	saloop

oo (o͞o)

bazooka
boomerang
kangaroo
macaroon
pantaloon
woomera
hooligan
bugaboo
koorajong
hullabaloo
hoochinoo
kookaburra
wanderoo

oo (o͝o)

book
foot
good
hook
moor
shook
stood
took
wool
brook

hood
poor
soot
boor
cook
crook
spoor
look
nook
wood
rook

manhood
mistook
backwoods
woodshed
woodruff
driftwood
cooky
cookbook
booklet
bookshelf
bookcase
scrapbook
textbook

crookneck
hooky
hookworm
fishhook
footstool
footrest
goodman
foot-loose
goodwill
footgear
mooring
woolfell
partook
woolpack

whippoorwill
underfoot
understood

VCV
hooka
afoot
betook
chinook
parenthood

171

sail	raid	glair	gaily
gain	waive	quaint	fairy
ail	rail	quail	abstain
aim	rain	gait	acclaim
Gail	wait	glaive	acquaint
frail	waist	praise	explain
air	wain	plait	exclaim
bail	raise	grail	entrails
flair	aid	grain	affair
flail	swain	strait	airplane
bait	wail	plaint	attain
baize	waif	plain	appraise
faith	vain	hail	entail
fair	saint	jail	disdain
bairn	slain	laird	daisy
braid	snail	cairn	daimen
faint	twain	paint	dairy
fain	trait	pain	contain
fail	train	Maine	assail
brail	chain	lair	chairman
brain	sprain	strain	bailiff
Cain	staid	braird	complain
braise	stain	maim	cocktail
drain	trail	Caird	daily
chaise	taint	maize	dainty

172

ai (ā)

glaiket
hangnail
Lorraine
impair
maintain
mermaid
Sinclair
sprigtail
terrain
obtain
sustain
waitress
ordain
pertain
wainscot
traitor
portrait
tailor
plaintiff
raiment
raisin
Convair
complaint
curtail
corsair

fingernail
entertain
appertain
hollandaise
scatterbrain

VCV
afraid
detain
declaim
avail
await
detail
despair
cocaine
restraint
domain
mohair
restrain
moraine
prevail
repair
remain
proclaim
refrain

regain
retail
retain
romaine

aileron
suzerain
remainder
polonaise
maintenance
chevrotain
legerdemain

-ain (ĭn)
final unaccented syllable
Britain
villain
bargain
captain
curtain
certain
chaplain
plantain
murrain
porcelain

173

Final ay

tray	splay	crayfish
bray	slay	crayon
chay	ray	crayman
clay	say	mayhap
day		Clayton
Fay	doomsday	maybe
flay	soothsay	Wayne
fray	estray	waylay
gay	hooray	rayon
gray	affray	playtime
hay	Thursday	mayhem
jay	subway	mayor
Kay	allay	playmate
lay	essay	plaything
may	birthday	
nay	array	mayonnaise
way	Sunday	
bay	portray	VCV
sway	parlay	
stay	Biscay	
stray	dismay	
pay	Bombay	
pray	<u>ch</u>ambray	
play	display	

VCV

Malay	betray
relay	delay
astray	defray
okay	decay
Friday	Saturday
belay	bayonet

ee   ea   oo   ai   ay

ooze	-	ease	swoop	-	sweep
bream		broom	steer		stair
cheer		chair	strait		street
fair		fear	beam		boom
heap		hoop	baize		booze
loop		leap	deem		doom
paid		pood	hoot		heat
poop		peep	leak		leek
see<u>the</u>		soo<u>the</u>	poon		pain
sloop		sleep	peak		peek
spook		speak	roof		reef
stoop		steep	shay		shoo
soot		seat	snool		snail
staid		steed	snook		sneak
swoon		swain	scoot		skeet
snooze		sneeze	spree		spray

brood - braid - breed   lair - leer - lear

steel	stool	steal	sain	soon	seen
weal	wail	wool	ween	wain	wean

oa (ō)

boat	loach	whoa	oakum
gloam	groat	toast	
bloat	hoarse	shoat	toadstool
boar	hoax	skoal	uproar
goat	hoar	Sloan	billboard
goal	hoard	road	cardboard
goad	groats	toad	roadster
gloat	roach	roam	charcoal
coarse	oath	roan	cockroach
foam	poach	throat	crossroad
foal	oak	stoat	railroad
float	oar	roar	inroad
croak	oats	roast	steamboat
board	Joan	soar	switchboard
boast	moat	soap	toadstone
cloak	moan	shoal	
groan	load	soak	**VCV**
broach	loaves		aboard
coach	loath	oatmeal	bezoar
coal	loathe	boatswain	afloat
coast	loam	approach	bemoan
coat	loan	encroach	reproach
coax	loaf	oarsman	cocoa
Zoar	toat	loafer	
shoad	woad	gloaming	petticoat

board - beard		rear - roar
bleat bloat		roost roast
coat coot		slain Sloan
loam loom		seek soak
loaves leaves		seep soap
reach roach		whoa whee
roan rain		cleek cloak

---

breech - broach - breach
boost beast boast
creak creek croak
gleam gloom gloam
hear hoar hair
meat moot moat
room ream roam
seam soom seem

oe (ō)

toe	roe	tiptoe	VCV
foe	doe	Roebuck	Defoe
Joe	sloe	Conroe	pekoe
floe	throe	Monroe	chigoe
goes	woe	Roscoe	Crusoe
hoe	Poe		oboe

ou (ou)

ouch	count	mouth	scout
bound	hound	pout	shout
mound	gouge	spout	pound
bouse	ground	mouse	scour
louse	crouch	noun	proud
bout	drouth	south	pounce
blouse	flout	sour	round
lounge	flour	our	rout
lout	gout	ours	souse
cloud	flounce	oust	tout
bounce	fount	grout	wound
loud	found	sound	vouch
jounce	foul	snout	trout
house	zounds	rouse	thou
clout	mount	slouch	trounce
couch	sprout	ounce	scrounge
pouch	out	shroud	douse

178

<u>ou</u> (ou)

espouse
discount
account
announce
expound
dumfound
astound
bounty
bounden
compound
confound
council
county
countess
counter
counsel
couchant
hellhound
founder
flounder
mountain
lousy
impound
fountain
foundry

outing
outline
thousand
titmouse
surround
surmount
scoundrel
penthouse
roundup
outwit
trousers
vouchsafe

accountant
boardinghouse
counterpane
thundercloud
counterpart
countinghouse
scoutmaster
outstanding
countermand
outlandish
countervail
customhouse

VCV

amount
aground
aloud
abound
about
around
avouch
arouse
carouse
renounce
devour
profound
devout
pronoun
pronounce
propound

boundary
tantamount
runabout
roundabout
paramount
bountiful
countenance
gadabout

ou (o͞o) (o͝o)

soup   bourd   accouter
wound   bouse   carrousel
pouf   gourde   Vancouver
group
croup   cougar   VCV
sou   louver   detour
you   goulash   douma
troupe   coupon   recoup
touse   congou   doura
nous   foulard   souter
dour   gourmand
coupe   tourist   touraco
rouge   uncouth   souvenir
your   Bourbon   troubadour
route   contour   noumenon
tour   Coulee   caribou
doum   Tournay   boulevard
bourg   yourself   acoustics
bourn   bourtree   tournament
bourse   bourdon   amadou
douce   nougat
youth   frou-frou   tour de force

ow (ou)

cow	crowd	trowel
bow	crown	towel
vow	fowl	tower
brow	frown	dowel
chow	gown	dower
wow	growl	flower
sow	howl	Howard
scow	drown	glower
row	down	power
plow		shower
prow	allow	prowess
how	endow	bowsprit
mow	dowdy	plowshare
ow	chowder	kow-tow
jow	cowry	pow-wow
now	dowry	
dowse	powder	howitzer
town	rowdy	safflower
scowl	dowy	
brown	drowsy	VCV
clown	frowsy	avow
prowl	bower	renoun
owl	coward	
jowl	cower	bowery
cowl	vowel	dowager

snow	elbow	bowl
bow	escrow	blown
crow	fallow	flown
flow	fellow	grown
glow	follow	growth
grow	furrow	shown
low	hallow	sown
mow	harrow	strown
own	hollow	thrown
row	marrow	bowleg
show	mellow	bowline
slow	minnow	crowbar
blow	morrow	
sow	narrow	Halloween
stow	pillow	marshmallow
strow	sallow	
throw	shallow	VCV
tow	sorrow	aglow
	sparrow	below
arrow	swallow	bestow
barrow	tallow	shadow
bellow	wallow	widow
borrow	willow	
whitlow	window	stowaway
	winnow	bungalow

Use only 1st reading response for digraphs; ea = (ē); oo = (o͞o); ou = (ou); ow = (ou)

beat - boot - bait - boat - beet - bout

pouch - peach - poach - pooch

sheet	shout	shoot	shoat
sour	sear	soar	seer
our	ear	air	oar

creed	- crood	- crowd	trait	- treat	- trout
louse	loose	lease	gain	goon	gown
float	fleet	flout	greet	groat	grout
roose	rouse	raise	gout	goat	gait
moose	mouse	maize	braise	browse	breeze
scoot	scout	skeet	oat	eat	out

cleat	- clout		root	- rout
crown	croon		snout	snoot
fount	faint		stoat	stout
flair	flour		sooth	south
growl	grail		tease	touse
noun	noon		couch	coach
peat	pout		coo	cow

au (au)

staunch	gaum	author
sauce	gaunt	August
cauld	daub	Austin
caul	claut	applause
auk	nautch	auburn
pause	maun	assault
maund	wauk	austere
Gaul	glaum	aural
haulm	waul	augur
paunch	whaup	augment
Paul	waur	audit
maul	taunt	bauxite
cause	vaunt	chauffer
clause	vault	Chaucer
launch	taut	gauffer
laud		hauberk
haunt	saucer	maunder
jaunt	dauntless	hausen
haul	Taurus	gauzy
haunch	maukin	caudal
fault	taurine	gaudy
faun	haunted	fausant
fraud	auxin	faunal
flaunt	applaud	cauldron
gauze	auto	gauntlet

laundress	saucy	aquanaut
laurel	Nassau	astronaut
laundry		auditor
launder	caulescent	overhaul
jaunty	Milwaukee	fraudulent
causal	authentic	aurora
caustic	tarpaulin	cauterize
faucet	autopsy	automat
dauphin	centaury	autograph
centaur	autumnal	autocrat
caudex	juggernaut	paucity
caucus		nautical
caulis	VCV	chaulmoogra
waukrife	Hausa	nautilus
hauberk	fauna	thesaurus
maumet	avaunt	traumatic
maudlin	Laura	dinosaur
plaudit	aura	holocaust
pauper	defraud	leprechaun
staumrel	because	
Faunus	debauch	authority
saunter	default	audacity
tautog	maraud	auditory
sausage	trauma	autonomy

185

aw (au)

saw	awl	jigsaw	pawpaw
craw	yaws	jackdaw	Lawrence
taw	awn	guffaw	Pawnee
straw	fawn	outlaw	Shawnee
claw	bawl	seesaw	tawdry
daw	drawn	withdraw	tawny
squaw	brawl	whipsaw	trawler
slaw	brawn	crawfish	rawhide
raw	dawn	awkward	mawkish
thraw	crawl	drawback	pawky
law	drawl	sawdust	
paw	thrawn	sawmill	awfully
maw	trawl	awful	strawberry
jaw	gawk	hawser	wapperjaw
haw	lawn	bawcock	unlawful
draw	hawk	bawty	wappen<u>ch</u>aw
flaw	yawn	awning	
caw	taws	bawbee	VCV
thaw	sprawl	gawsy	pashaw
blaw	squawk	drawer	Mackinaw
braw	pawn	hawthorn	Catawba
chaw	spawn	sawyer	overawe
shaw	shawl	lawyer	tomahawk
staw	prawn	awlwort	Chickasaw
awe	scrawl	goshawk	Mohawk

<u>oi</u> (oi)

coil
boil
groin
hoise
hoicks
moil
poi
broil
poise
choice
point
coif
oil
poind
coin
noise
moist
foin
foist
loin
joist
foil
hoist
joint
join

void
quoit
roil
voile
voice
spoil
soil
toil

cancroid
cloistress
grabboid
adjoin
exploit
appoint
algoid
enjoin
doily
foison
embroil
broiler
goiter
discoid
deltoid
cloister

invoice
haploid
hypnoid
histoid
moidore
mattoid
sainfoin
joinder
loiter
oilcloth
moisture
mastoid
oilskin
parboil
poison
ointment
l'envoi
purloin
sirloin
standpoint
scincoid
subsoil
turquoise
tinfoil
turmoil

tabloid

sphygmoid

borzoi

celloiiden

hoi polloi

ellipsoid

molluscoid

counterfoil

tenderloin

counterpoint

colloidal

concoidal

embroider

VCV

recoil

placoid

anoint

avoid

meloid

aroid

aroint

devoid

adroit

troika

typhoid

trefoil

thyroid

gadoid

keloid

globoid

hydroid

haloid

rejoice

theroid

sparoid

apheroid

carangoid

asteroid

metaloid

adenoid

alkaloid

trapezoid

paranoid

anthropoid

celluloid

reconnoiter

hoity-toity

boy

foy

Roy

Choy

joy

Troy

cloy

toy

coy

hoy

soy

Lloyd

sloyd

Floyd

tomboy

alloy

enjoy

annoy

employ

charpoy

convoy

envoy

carboy

cowboy

foyer

loyal

voyage

royal

boycott

oyster

hoyden

boyhood

coypu

gargoyle

disloyal

flamboyant

clairvoyance

boysenberry

VCV

savoy

destroy

ahoy

deploy

decoy

corduroy

unemployment

ee ea oo ai oa oe ou ow au aw oi oy

Use first reading response for vowel digraphs.

foul	feel	fool	fail	foal	fowl	foil
	teel	toil	tool	tail	teal	
	eel	owl	awl	oil	ail	
	tee	too	taw	toy	tea	

chaise	choose	cheese	choice
foin	fain	fawn	faun
groan	groin	grain	green
cowl	coil	coal	cool
Troy	tray	tree	true
roil	rail	real	reel

soil	seal	sail	bawl	boil	bail
Joan	Jean	join	coon	coin	Cain
brail	brawl	broil	pause	poise	pease

foist	-	feast		joust	-	joist
noose		noise		paint		point

192

Adam Choy

L.W.: would bald

Adam Anders Authur Choy
Doused his food with sauce of soy –
Rouked and prouked and sprouked his floif
With catsup, stouch, and oil of oif.
He peppered and soused a stoig of cherry –
Then slinked to his bunk, feeling very un-merry.
His stashing stopped. He felt no joy.
(No more foul filling for Adam Choy!)

Mr. Troil

"Do sit on the couch," said Mrs. Ouch.
"I've troum in a grouz to feed you!
I'll fill your sprouch
And drix your drouch,
And, since you're bald, I'll seed you."

"Oh, thank you, Mam," said Mr. Troil.
"You toil in vain. Don't spoil me!
I've oix to dip,
And broive to sip,
And hair on my pate would spoil me!"

Shaun

"How brave I am," said Shaun, the clown.
"How sloil and slaush and sleet!"
With that, he loiched and dauched his zoun
And sloiged his staubby feet!

193

ue (ū) (o͞o)

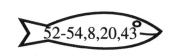

blue	tissue
clue	undue
cue	vendue
due	virtue
flue	issue
glue	Tuesday
hue	Purdue
rue	
sue	
true	
slue	VCV
grue	

	statue
accrue	revue
argue	value
construe	ague
endue	venue
ensue	
fondue	revenue
imbue	avenue
pursue	residue
rescue	barbecue
subdue	retinue
fescue	continue

ie (ē)

priest	tier	goalie
bield	mien	eerie
bier	lien	Lassie
wield	lief	dowie
thieve		Barbie
brief	Scottie	ganzie
chief	bawtie	swelchie
thief	baukie	Maggie
siege	clootie	crappie
spiel	hoodie	cashier
fief	Margie	Algiers
field	pardie	Diesel
shriek	pixie	gambier
shield	sortie	piedmont
fiend	zombie	wiener
fierce	birdie	windshield
yield	brownie	shieling
pierce	rookie	
pier	pyxie	glockenspiel
frieze	collie	chesterfield
grief	cookie	Piedmontest
piece	prairie	outfielder
niece	laddie	handkerchief
grieve	Dixie	heebie-jeebies
liege	Elsie	boogie woogie

(ie) (ē) VCV ie (ī)

retrieve	pie	cried
reprieve	tie	pried
achieve	die	tried
believe	lie	dried
dogie	fie	fried
relief	hie	shied
premier	vie	spied
hygiene		lied
rabies		
series	fiery	
Marie	pieplant	
stogie	magpie	
genie	applied	
mashie	complied	

reverie	VCV	
brigadier	belie	
calorie		
jardiniere	satisfied	
<u>ch</u>andelier	dignified	
cavalier	qualified	
	certified	
electrolier	occupied	
menagerie		

– Sloan, the Sportsman –

Sloan felt <u>moon</u> <u>moan</u> mean,
Nerves were <u>fraud</u> <u>freed</u> frayed.
He had <u>choo</u> <u>chaw</u> chow,
Then down <u>load</u> <u>loud</u> laid.

"I'll get <u>oat</u> <u>eat</u> out!
Fun is <u>day</u> <u>doe</u> due.
Golf I'll <u>ploy</u> <u>plea</u> play –
That's the <u>claw</u> <u>cloy</u> clue!"

Game was <u>spooled</u> <u>spieled</u> spoiled –
Rain and <u>heal</u> <u>haul</u> hail!
He got <u>bout</u> <u>beat</u> boat,
So's to <u>seal</u> <u>soil</u> sail.

Lines were <u>toot</u> <u>tout</u> taut,
But no <u>braise</u> <u>browse</u> breeze.
Boat rammed <u>pair</u> <u>poor</u> pier,
Then came <u>bays</u> <u>boys</u> bees!

Sloan fixed <u>real</u> <u>rail</u> reel
With his <u>teal</u> <u>tail</u> tool,
But his <u>trait</u> <u>treat</u> trout
Jumped in <u>pail</u> <u>peal</u> pool!

Note well: Read through for meaning first, omitting the underlined words!

"I'll go <u>sheet</u> <u>shout</u> shoot!"
Aimed at <u>joy</u> <u>jaw</u> jay.
Hit just <u>oar</u> <u>our</u> air
All the <u>due</u> <u>doe</u> day!

Butts by <u>gait</u> <u>gout</u> goat –
Up a <u>tray</u> <u>true</u> tree!
Down he <u>skeeted</u> <u>scouted</u> scooted –
What a <u>spry</u> <u>spray</u> spree!

Sat and <u>bailed</u> <u>boiled</u> bawled,
Nursed his <u>poon</u> <u>pawn</u> pain.
Sipped root <u>boar</u> <u>boor</u> beer.
"I lack <u>brawn</u> <u>brown</u> brain!"

M-m-m-m!

Dapper Danny fattens misses
As he passes candy kisses!

R<u>ea</u>dy, Team? Y<u>ea</u>!

Give the Rockets <u>chair</u> <u>choor</u> cheer!
Laud them loud and <u>cloar</u> <u>clair</u> clear!
Pound that Panther <u>fee</u> <u>foo</u> foe.
Till Rockets roar and <u>gay</u> <u>gow</u> go!

ei (ē)   ei (ā)

weird   feint
Neil   beige
Keith   seine
weir   sei<u>ch</u>e
sheik   lei
seize   Seine
               veil
ceiling   vein
seizure   their
perceive   rein
caffeine   skein
leisure
neither   reindeer
either   checkrein
conceive   chow mein
conceit
Neiman's   surveillance

VCV
receive   VCV
codeine   geisha
deceit   obeisance
deceive
protein

199

ey (ē) 🔑

key	chutney	Sydney
	donkey	volley
pulley	chimney	Wesley
abbey	gooey	valley
parley	cockney	turkey
parsley	jersey	tourney
murrey	galley	trolley
osprey	hackney	charley horse
alley	jitney	
barley	Kinsey	
mulley	dinkey	**VCV**
motley	spinney	jockey dickey
lamprey	Whitney	lackey rickey
blarney	Shirley	hickey baloney
medley	whiskey	Odyssey hockey
kidney	surrey	hokey-pokey
Hershey	Barney	

<u>eu</u> (ū)

Zeus
leud
deuce
feu
sleuth
feud

Steuben
Reuben
Zeuxis
Eugene
Eurus
Euclid
neuter
euphroe
neutral
neuron
feudal
eusol
neural
eucaine
euclase

eupeptic
euplastic

heulandite
heuristic
eurythmy
eutectic

VCV
euthenics
Eu<u>ch</u>arist
euripus
euphemism
eureka
eulogy
euphony
neuritis
eugenics
neurotic
maneuver
Teutonic
deutoplasm
therapeutic
eucalyptus
neurologist

Deuteronomy
pharmaceutical

201

ew (ū) (o͞o)

pew	stew	span-new
phew	whew	newel
mewl	tew	Lewis
blew	yew	mildew
brew	skew	newborn
spew	thew	withdrew
slew	shrewd	sewage
chew	screw	skewer
crew	shrew	sewer
newt	strew	outgrew
mew	threw	newsboy
new		newsreel
dew	fewtrils	pewter
ewe	fitchew	steward
drew	Andrew	dewlap
grew	curlew	
few	jewel	VCV
lewd	dewdrop	sinew
Jew	churchpew	askew
hewn	ewer	cashew
flew	curfew	nephew
hew	crewel	renew
thews	Agnew	review

Phew!

Reuben sandwich for supper, and too much ice
    cream
Gave me hard, hapless night, and this long,
    lurid dream.

Andrew, Lewis and I, greedy pals, were to
    swallow
The bad brew, the weird stew, whose contents
    now follow:
Six sinews of shrew, a mammal that's wee,
Detached tail of newt, (salamander is he!)
A curlew's curved bill, and black dice thrown
      as deuce;
Cashew nuts, shelled and chewy, and a statue of
    Zeus;
Yew branches, new-hewn, from those evergreen
    trees;
Three photos of sideburns, crew cuts and
    goatees;
Eucalyptus oil fragrant, a dewlap of cow;
Slews of screws that had mildew, and left ear of
    sow;
Three tendrils of the wand'ring Jew plant that I
    grew;

Powdered horn of a ram, bits of wool from
    a ewe –
Were dampened with dewdrops (clear jewels
    from a willow!)
And mixed in a bowl set on crewel-stitched
    pillow,
Then spewed into pitcher, a fine pewter
    ewer!
Pals drank the concoction. WE WERE TWO
BOYS FEWER!!
Electrons and protons and neutrons and such
Were strewn on the pew. Farewell, twins I
    liked much!
Quite scared, I delivered a eulogy fine.
(Deuteronomy helped – 31:29!*)

Eureka, I woke! The maneuver? I'd dreamt
    it!
But sleep after feast? I'll not soon reattempt
    it!

*"Ye will utterly corrupt yourselves."

<u>ee</u> <u>ea</u> <u>oo</u> <u>ai</u> <u>ay</u> <u>oa</u> <u>oe</u> <u>ou</u> <u>ow</u> <u>au</u>

<u>aw</u> <u>oi</u> <u>oy</u> <u>eu</u> <u>ue</u> <u>ie</u> <u>ei</u> <u>ew</u> <u>ey</u>

loud   laud   lead   lewd
laid   load   Lloyd   leud

flaw   flay   flee   flue   flew   floe   flea
lien   lain   loan   loin   lean   lawn   loon
pow   pew   paw   pay   pea   Poo   poi

Reid   road   reed   raid   read   rood
rue   raw   Roy   roe   row   ray
loo   lea   Lew   law   lee   lay
few   feu   fee   foe   foy   Fay
chaw   chew   chow   choo   Choy   chay

broo   brow   bray   bree   brew
mean   mien   moon   main   moan
Joy   Joe   jaw   Jew   jay

spoil   speel   spool   spiel
pier   poor   pair   peer
<u>th</u>ow   <u>th</u>ee   thaw   thew

ee ea oo ai ay oa oe ou ow au
aw oi oy eu ue ie ei ew ey

boor   bier   boar   beer

now   new   nay   Noo

loof   loaf   leif   leaf

Neal   Neil   nail

feud   food   feed

grieve   groove

crew   craw

tear   tier

sheik   shook

scree   screw

found   friend

clue   cloy   claw   clay   clew

how   hay   hoy   hue   haw

toe   tee   tie   taw   too

206

ui (o͞o)	ey (ā)	
juice	trey	convey
bruise	grey	survey
suit	they	purvey
sluice	whey	
bruit	prey	Monterrey
cruise	hey	
fruit	fley	VCV
	gley	obey
nuisance	wey	
suitor		
pursuit		
VCV		
recruit		

The Monterrey Maid

The steward had a maid in pursuit
As she sipped whey and juice of a fruit.
"He's a nuisance, this suitor!
Bruit the news of this brute, or
I'll disembark cruise and bring suit!"

207

-<u>ous</u> (ŭs)

-<u>ous</u> may be the final syllable of a base word or it may be a suffix meaning "full of."

<u>ous</u> as a suffix:

pompous

joyous

phosphorous

ponderous

murderous

poisonous

mountainous

marvelous

prosperous

thunderous

traitorous

scandalous

slanderous

cancerous

ulcerous

vigorous

glamorous

humorous

hazardous

vaporous

rigorous

libelous

cavernous

viperous

clamorous

<u>ous</u> as an ending (or irregularly-added suffix):

j<u>ea</u>lous

mucous

monstrous

lustrous

fibrous

nitrous

leprous

viscous

raucous

fuscous

h<u>ei</u>nous

tremendous

stupendous

fabulous

ravenous

nebulous

tr<u>ea</u>cherous

numerous

populous

credulous

querulous

timorous

ludicrous

ominous

tremulous

lecherous

molluscous

miraculous

unanimous

monotonous

homogenous

preposterous

obstreperous

felicitous

polygamous

208

A flea and a fly in a flue

Were imprisoned, so what did they do?

Said the flea, "Let us fly!"

Said the fly, "Let us flee!"

So they flew out a flaw in the flue.

Boo Bookworm is glad, and he beams,

For he likes to chomp paper in reams.

He'll excitedly roam,

For each tome is a home,

And each page is a room, so it seems!

A man put his fowl up for sale.

"Your clucking is more like a wail!

You must feel very foul

To foil even a foal!

It's a fool's trick you play, and you fail!"

Use the most common pronunciation, the first reading response.

* *

ain	kew	joace	scoy
toint	prause	sclow	greal
choag	haind	splaud	cheesp
droe	squay	croy	chauf
quait	jaush	oud	quoak
prouch	eun	swoan	phray
teud	snue	veul	spraig
scue	scawl	ainge	ploage
caun	twoy	proug	ceag
slaup	loaz	froist	troist
vaw	coaf	scaib	claup
hoag	glound	tue	droust
proid	goil	aux	boit
froace	jeun	shauce	crauch
phrout	seab	ceif	queel
loint	sclay	smow	roace
dwien	throace	scray	claig
chaist	traige	neub	graif
proange	moaf	snauth	nean
quoip	proy	splaw	troust
yoy	eace	lieb	snoy
thue	cleek	caush	beul
doul	taug	taisp	dieve
graw	laup	bew	deet

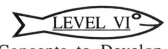

Concepts to Develop

Page	Letter Order	
213	o (ŭ)	Reading schwa sound in accented syl. Irregular for reading and spelling
214	al (aul)	Regular medial and final spelling in one-syl. word
215	eigh (ā) igh (ī)	Irregular for spelling Irregular for spelling
217	ind-old	"Kind-old" words
218	-ble, -dle, -tle, etc.	Final stable syl., part of base word, never acented, lacks vowel sound. Sound picture = (b'l), etc. Careful pronunciation <u>b'l</u> like blend <u>bl</u>, not (bŭl). <u>zle</u> Regular for spelling (z'l) <u>puzzle</u>
221	ckle (k'l)	Regular for spelling after short vowel in 2-syl. word <u>buckle.</u> <u>cle</u> (k'l) Regular for spelling in three and more syl. words.
222	stle (s'l)	Regular for spelling (s'l) <u>whistle</u>
224	Medial <u>ck</u>	Regular for spelling after a short V, and before <u>e</u>, <u>i</u>, or <u>y</u>

225	V/V	V/V syllable division between two vowels.
		  1. which do not combine to form digraph or dipthong. li´on
		  2. which usually combine to form digraph or dipthong. cre/ate´
		(These two syl. division principles are introduced in <u>ANGLING WORKBOOK.</u>

	<u>ANGLING WORKBOOK</u> p. 96. When the final letter in a b.w. is the same as the first letter of a suffix, double consonants occur; however, a triple consonant is not allowed without a hyphen: mean = ness = <u>meanness</u> full = ly = <u>fully</u> or <u>ful-ly</u>	
228	tion (shŭn)	Final stable syl. Practice reading <u>tion</u> as (shŭn), not (sh) (ŭn) (am bi´ shun) not (ambish´un) Syl. before <u>shun</u> receives primary accent. <u>i</u> is short at end of accented syl. before <u>tion</u>; all other vowels are long in this situation. con dĭ´ tion com plē´tion Complete review of all syl. division. Rhythm is helpful in pronouncing long words. Note pattern before each list. <u>tion</u> is regular spelling of (shŭn)

Page	Letter Order	Concepts to Develop (Cont'd.)
236	sion (shŭn)	<u>sion</u> behaves as <u>tion</u> Irregular for spelling
	sion (zhŭn)	<u>sion</u> behaves as <u>tion</u> Regular for spelling
236	sion (shŭn) (zhŭn)	Auditory drills in distinguishing between (shŭn) and (zhŭn) may be necessary
238	ant ance ancy ent ence ency	Careful pronunciation is the key to spelling these words. <u>ance</u>, <u>ence</u> are regularly spelled with <u>c</u> Final (sĭ) is regularly spelled <u>cy</u>.
239	ary ery ory	<u>ary</u> is regular spelling for (ĕr´ĭ)
240		A suffix may change pronunciation of a b.w. <u>ma´jor</u> <u>major´ity</u>
242	Silent letters	Irregular for spelling
244	ear, our (ûr)	Irregular for spelling
245	-ine (ĭn) ice (ĭs), etc.	Irregular for spelling Occasionally V-<u>e</u> does not cause a long vowel sound.
246	-ture (cho͞or) tu (cho͞o)	Regular for spelling final syl. of multi-syl words. Regular for medial spelling in multi-syl words. <u>century</u>
247	i (y)	Regular for spelling in final syl. <u>union</u>
248	Final (sh) syl.	<u>ti</u>, <u>ci</u>, <u>si</u>, <u>ce</u>, <u>se</u> may combine with vowels to form final syls. (shȧ) (shăl) (shŭs) (shăn) (shĕnt) (zhȧ) (zhăn) Final <u>ci</u> <u>ate</u> and <u>ti</u> <u>ate</u> = (shĭ āt) <u>appreciate</u> These (sh) syls. parallel the <u>tions</u>. They must be read as a whole: (ambi´shus) not (am bish´us); the syl. before (sh) receives the primary accent; <u>i</u> preceding (sh) is short. <u>initial</u> (ĭ nĭ´ shăl) List words are arranged by length and the accent is regular. Rhythmic reading will facilitate pronunciation. It is helpful to put common (sh) syls. on cards to be read frequently until student is familiar with the syls.
252	(ī) (ā)	Occasionally <u>i</u> and <u>a</u> take a long sound at the end of an unaccented syl. ī de´ a or ā or´ ta
253		Confusing words. Read carefully!

o (ŭ) in accented syllable

won	Monday	nothing
come	monkey	stoma<u>ch</u>
ton	wonder	covey
dove	affront	
done	frontage	governor
sponge		somersault
shove	color	wonderful
dost	bro<u>th</u>er	honeymoon
monk	mo<u>th</u>er	discover
front	cover	coverture
some	smo<u>th</u>er	coverlet
from	honey	government
none	dozen	cover-point
month	covet	
son	govern	VCV
love	sloven	among
glove	hover	above
	shovel	become
comfort	covert	amongst
confront	hovel	company
compass	plover	ano<u>th</u>er
frontier	oven	recover
pommel	o<u>th</u>er	accompany
London	money	

213

al (aul)

In one-syl. words, an <u>a</u> followed by <u>l</u> is regularly pronounced (au).

Spelling help: (aul) is regularly spelled <u>al</u> or <u>all</u> in one-syl words.

ball	small	pall	halt
all	squall	thrall	malt
call	stall	wall	scald
gall	tall	bald	salt
hall		false	waltz

In multisyllable words, <u>al</u> is more often pronounced (ăl); however, <u>l</u> occasionally influences the sound of <u>a</u>:

almost	exalt	alr<u>ea</u>dy
also	palfrey	almighty
always	stalwart	alderman
appall	halter	alternate
alter	asphalt	gyrfalcon
altar	caldron	VCV
palsy	falter	cobalt
paltry	Maltese	balsa
balsam	Baltic	almanac
Balkan	maltose	subaltern

Winter, spring,
Summer, fall.
These are the seasons –
Four in all.

eigh (ā)

eight

weigh

freight

weight

neigh

sleigh

freighter

eighteen

eighty

neighbor

inveigh

neighborhood

---

igh (ī)

light

bight

high

blight

fright

bright

flight

fight

thigh

tight

might

night

slight

sigh

plight

sight

right

mighty

nightmare

sprightly

spotlight

highness

torchlight

highway

flashlight

moonlight

VCV

delight

twilight

As you pronounce the following nonsense words, use the most common sound for each digraph. You will recognize a real word.

1. aik
2. nier
3. theeph
4. scool
5. blaid
6. deight
7. whight
8. broot
9. whiel
10. haist
11. phait
12. plaice
13. broak
14. phiet
15. yoo
16. steight
17. groe
18. drigh
19. reud
20. biech
21. fliet
22. leight
23. cight
24. wiek

25. reut
26. woond
27. loe
28. preigh
29. saik
30. smaul
31. soop
32. croe
33. ceik
34. scraip
35. neece
36. phligh
37. bloo
38. triet
39. ried
40. beerd
41. caip
42. voat
43. sweigh
44. sheeld
45. naim
46. sloap
47. fraize
48. snoe

49. miet
50. bigh
51. phloe
52. liek
53. ceit
54. spreigh
55. sprigh
56. bloe
57. phloo
58. nue
59. ceim
60. meight
61. braik
62. waige
63. pigh
64. choo
65. lieph
66. staik
67. poak
68. greight
69. staul
70. criep
71. reigh
72. doam

In one-syllable words, <u>i</u> and <u>o</u> sometimes take the long sound before two consonants.

kind	old	boll	volt
bind	gold	roll	molt
blind	hold	poll	smolt
wind	scold	toll	dolt
mind	told	droll	don't
grind	fold	troll	won't
hind	bold	scroll	both
rind	cold	stroll	loth
find	host	bolt	sloth
wild	most	colt	Christ
child	post	jolt	pint
mild			

In these common words, <u>a</u> is long before two consonants:

āche	taste	danger
change	paste	stranger
range	waste	manger
mange	baste	ranger
grange	haste	granger
strange	chaste	āngel

217

ble, etc., syllables are final stable syllables which stick together.
le takes the consonant before it, and this syllable is never accented.

To read, cover the ble, etc., and sound out first syllable. To spell, spell the first
syllable and add ble, etc.

Note: (z´l) is regularly spelled zlë.

an´|gle	pŭd´|dle	title	scuttle
rumble	apple	tittle	quibble
jungle	bubble	noble	whiffle
pimple	cripple	hobble	baffle
tangle	dabble	riffle	table
simple	nipple	rifle	stable
temple	rattle	gable	babble
humble	juggle	gabble	nettle
bungle	little	paddle	cable
fumble	wiggle	padle	dribble
dimple	battle	ruble	twiddle
bundle	middle	rubble	cuddle
mingle	gobble	cattle	drizzle
marble	bottle	pebble	maple
jumble		raffle	nozzle
ramble	fā´|ble	muddle	muffle
garble	bugle	staple	smuggle
candle	idle	huddle	poodle
gamble	able	coddle	scruple
handle	cradle	stifle	griddle
amble	trifle	dapple	whittle

noodle	stiffle	mufle	cudle
muzzle	rafle	sadle	uzzle
puzzle	catle	criple	rettle
Bible	mapple	tabble	tatle
haggle	wiffle	yoddle	gogle
mumble	rufle	strugle	neddle
ruffle	siddle	hoble	eggle
bauble	wagle	buble	bable
kettle	snifle	briddle	shufle
foible	abble	ridle	jogle
sable	batle	twidle	fizle
ample	stragle	triffle	muzle
foozle	jugle	hudle	fetle
toddle	buggle	drible	miggle
ladle	stapple	laddle	dazle
gargle	botle	iddle	aple
bridle	litle	wigle	hagle
gaggle	ratle	midle	codle
tattle	pable	drizle	gridle
ogle	stabble	puzle	pudle
doodle	goble	labble	kiddle
giggle	badle	stradle	niple
sizzle	craddle	stepple	dable
tumble	fidle	mudle	adle
sidle	fabble	nozle	opple

-ble, -dle, -tle, etc.

rectangle

assemble

carbuncle

embezzle

example

quadrangle

encircle

bamboozle

dissemble

kenspeckle

article

barnacle

entitle

disciple

binnacle

canticle

popsicle

skimble-scamble

fiddle-faddle

jingle-jangle

ignoble

inveigle

spectacle

quintuple

principle

fascicle

obstacle

tentacle

pinnacle

ventricle

multiple

quadruple

particle

chronicle

bernicle

pellicle

caulicle

miracle

soluble

vehicle

coracle

icicle

monocle

finagle

cuticle

oracle

manacle

voluble

tubercle

resemble

tricycle

vesicle

cubicle

bicycle

bedraggle

calycle

motorcycle

receptacle

honeysuckle

participle

mollycoddle

wallydraigle

Constantinople

220

buckle ruckle twinkle
pickle mickle crankle
freckle shackle sprinkle
chuckle suckle skinkle
tickle cackle ankle
crackle hackle sparkle
fickle sickle tinkle
tackle strickle snorkle
trickle mackle
speckle truckle -<u>cle</u>
cockle
brickle -<u>kle</u> treacle
grackle circle
heckle rankle uncle
prickle crinkle cycle
muckle socle

<u>Pie, O My!</u>

<u>H</u>-<u>u</u> huckle, <u>b</u>-<u>u</u> buckle, <u>h</u>-<u>u</u> huckle <u>y</u>.
<u>H</u>-<u>u</u> huckle, <u>b</u>-<u>u</u> buckle, huckleberry pie!

<u>Chew</u>berry, <u>dew</u>berry, <u>glue</u>berry – Yi!
<u>Mew</u>berry, <u>new</u>berry, <u>blue</u>berry pie!

Read first, pronouncing silent letters.

bristle	nestle	wrestle
bustle	pestle	apostle
castle	justle	epistle
gristle	rustle	
hustle	thistle	muscle
jostle	whistle	corpuscle
trestle	throstle	subtle

Pronounce final syllable plainly:

label	Bible	marvel
table	libel	marble
nimble	opal	vandal
symbol	ogle	handle
coddle	eagle	fatal
model	legal	maple
rebel	frugal	jostle
pebble	bugle	fossil
gospel	chortle	peddle
stopple	mortal	pedal

222

mussel	tassel	castle
muscle	tussle	vassal
missal	vessel	gerbil
whistle	nestle	verbal
noble	gristle	idle
global	tinsel	idol

Pronounce carefully:*

-stle, -scle (s´l)

Jim's epistle told of the hustle and bustle of the big city and of his trip to the suburbs. "My train whistled as it jostled over a trestle which was bristling with thistle. Soon an old castle, nestling in the wooded hills, could be seen. The apostles of reform are wrestling with plans to rustle out the overgrown grounds and to sell private lots. They will muscle in with a subtle, quiet setting for all to enjoy. Its club house at the end of the golf course will be named, at my suggestion, the Subtle Tee."

*Read once, pronouncing silent letters as a spelling aid; then reread.

Spelling helps:
 <u>k</u> seldom occurs after a short vowel. If (k) follows a short vowel and falls
 before <u>e</u>, <u>i</u>, or <u>y</u>, <u>ck</u> must be used.

bucket	hickey	stricken
cricket	hockey	Dickens
docket	jockey	chicken
jacket	lackey	bracken
locket	Stuckey	
packet	dickey	
picket	rickey	wacky
pocket		tacky
racket	bicker	stocky
rocket	cracker	Kentucky
rickets	checker	
socket	dicker	
sprocket	flicker	ticking
thicket	slicker	stocking
ticket	locker	rickie
wicket	snicker	nickel
fecket	wicker	
Becket	pucker	
rickety	crockery	
bracket	mackerel	Mackinaw
Crockett	pickerel	mackintosh

Two adjacent vowels which do not form a digraph must divide.

These words can be divided regularly in only one way. Only the accent must be determined.

an'nu|al
tri'an|gle
cardiac
champion
Indian
scorpion
Pontiac
liable
actual
Borneo
vitreous
raffia
virtual

factual
obvious
Caspian
congruous
galleon
bounteous
arduous
igneous
Thespian
plenteous
pantheon

diagnose

alliance
Rialto

centennial
septennial
millennium
adverbial
insomnia
accordion
asphyxia

terrestrial
contemptuous

Final syllable takes consonant before it.

di'a|mond
creosote
hyacinth
iodine
peony
theory
violent

dialect
eosin
diocese
leotard
diadem
dialyze
Siamese

diaper
diary
violet
violate
leonine
viaduct
theorem

violin
pioneer
viola

geography
theocracy
bibliography

VV

Dividing Between Vowels Which Do Not Form Digraphs or Dipthongs

Dividing words with VC/CV + V/V formulas should now be automatic.
Each of the following words also contains one VCV syl. division choice.

<u>Goliath</u>:   Gō´li ath   Gŏl´i ath   Gŏ lī´ath

cameo	vacuum	pedestrian
caviar	trivial	conspicuous
meteor	radium	proverbial
manual	idiot	eventual
idiom	oriole	Corinthian
hideous	jovial	Olympiad
chariot	tedious	colloquial
clarion	mediate	spontaneous
folio	stadium	barbarian
genial	menial	wisteria
mania	myriad	Ontario
casual	podium	symposium
lariat	zodiac	magnesium
helium	serial	Mongolia

V/V

Two vowels which usually form digraphs may divide.

___ ___ ´ ___   ___ ´ ___ ___

fiesta	terrier	Orient
meander	nausea	barrier
museum	alien	
mosaic	atheist	___ ___ ___ ´
heroic	cereal	Soviet
oasis	lenient	Vietnam
sienna	preamble	reinforce
theatric	scientist	Juliet
prosaic	permeate	minuet
Vienna	heroin	___ ___ ´ ___ ___
siesta	area	coordinate
Balboa	altruism	cooperate
Sierra	nucleus	ingredient
duello	suicide	linoleum
duenna	furrier	obedient
archaic	laity	variety
		coagulate

-tion (shŭn)

1. The syl. before (shŭn) takes the primary accent.

stā|tion	suction	sanction
action	faction	fraction
caption	lotion	auction
diction	caution	nation
junction	friction	section
notion	option	function
fiction	potion	ration
portion	traction	unction
mention	motion	

2. One consistent irregularity is: i before (shŭn) is always short.
   All other vowels are long.

ad|dĭ|tion	collection	insertion
ambition	conception	perdition
commotion	cognition	contortion
completion	contraction	conjunction
pollution	assertion	corruption
starvation	confection	addiction
condition	inscription	formation
dictation	injection	foundation
carnation	sensation	ablution
ignition	conviction	consumption
temptation	conduction	contrition
excretion	inspection	infraction
partition	inflation	extraction

228

cor|rec|tion

attraction

extortion

frustration

extinction

subscription

concretion

contraption

distinction

plantation

affection

assumption

construction

infection

taxation

exaction

fixation

attention

convention

indention

induction

conscription

instruction

compunction

oblation

distortion

diffraction

infliction

narration

disruption

abstraction

absorption

dysfunction

translation

abduction

exemption

perfection

intention

invention

accretion

objection

inflection

dissection

injunction

subjunction

obstruction

affliction

distraction

cessation

dentition

apportion

subjection

salvation

subtraction

damnation

exertion

transition

absention

contention

gestation

tion (chŭn) after s:

question

suggestion

ingestion

bastion

congestion

combustion

a|dop´|tion   promotion   prevention
donation   precaution   presumption
deduction   desertion   proportion
emotion   ligation   duration
detection   locution   production
relation   dejection   projection
solution   rejection   resumption
rotation   selection   decoction
tradition   deception   defection
devotion   probation   redemption
election   detention   eruption
quotation   edition   volition
reduction   position   protection
reception   vocation   sedition
notation   ovation   sedation
location   legation   mutation
munition   petition   oration

---

nu|tri´|tion   reflection   detraction
secretion   protraction   description
destruction   prescription   proscription

V/V

tu|i´|tion   reaction
fruition   creation

in|ter|rup|tion
conversation
cancellation
transportation
consummation
indentation
illustration
information
fermentation
constellation
conservation
intervention
confirmation
consultation
confiscation
observation
expectation
compensation
affectation
condensation
interjection
affirmation
exportation
annexation
consternation

concentration
dispensation
distillation
assignation
insurrection
commendation
dissertation
incantation
oscillation
perturbation
transformation
ostentation
exultation
condemnation
malformation
indignation
importation
exhortation
contemplation
exploitation
apperception
circumspection
incarnation
appellation
conformation

Reading help for long words:
The vowel before <u>tion</u> regularly takes the consonant before it.

com´ pĕ ti´ tion   (<u>not</u> com pĕt i´ tion)

ac´ cŭ sa´ tion   (<u>not</u> ac cŭs a´ tion)

suf´ fŏ ca´ tion   (<u>not</u> suf fŏc a´ tion)

con´ trả dic´ tion   (<u>not</u> con trăd ic´ tion)

However, the vowel before <u>tion</u> does not take an <u>r</u> from the <u>er</u> combination.

des´ per a´ tion

---

in|stĭ|tu´|tion

opposition

expedition

disposition

distribution

constitution

persecution

imposition

application

calculation

cultivation

congregation

destination

corporation

introduction

consolation

exclamation

implication

exploration

indication

expiration

admiration

combination

fascination

inspiration

irrigation

proclamation

restoration

syncopation

vaccination

obligation

innovation

connotation

conjugation

formulation

reclamation

dem´|on|stra´|tion*
hi´|ber|na´|tion
designation
preservation
liberation
prolongation
relaxation
protestation
legislation
presentation
jurisdiction
federation
recollection
satisfaction
recognition
superstition
resignation
registration
devastation
operation
adaptation
detestation
resurrection
retardation
reservation

deportation
inundation
usurpation
aberration
abolition
locomotion
toleration
isolation
limitation
liquidation
desolation
elevation
moderation
education
domination
benediction
definition
delegation
numeration
decoration
agitation
adoration
coronation
elocution
veneration

*de´mon stra´ tion   <u>dem´on stra´tion</u>

VCV __ ´__ __ za´tion

civ|il|i|za´|tion
humanization
localization
equalization
modernization
legalization
memorization
vocalization
polarization
sterilization
utilization
stabilization
vaporization
unitization
vitalization
paralyzation
mobilization
colonization
moralization
minimization
penalization
fraternization
glamorization
idolization
me<u>ch</u>anization

VCV __ ´__ fi ca´tion

notification
gratification
purification
qualification
clarification
ratification
modification
unification
verification
glorification
pacification
edification
ramification
specification
vilification
codification

---

recommendation
regimentation
manifestation
juxtaposition
presupposition
representation

234

6-syllable

__ __ ´__ __ __ ´tion

experimentation
disqualification
intensification
exemplification
personification
electrification
solidification
diversification
saponification
homogenization
demoralization
monopolization
transistorization

__ ´__ __ __ za´tion

capitalization
liberalization
mineralization
naturalization
characterization
generalization
hospitalization

militarization
alphabetization
popularization
rehabilitation
excommunication
prestidigitation
tintinnabulation

V/V __ ´__ __ __ a´tion

mutualization
visualization
reconciliation

Americanization
industrialization
memorialization
demilitarization
materialization

8-syllable

intellectualization

-<u>sion</u> (shŭn)

man̍|sion
passion
mission
pension
session
torsion
tension
fission
cession

con|fes̍|sion
admission
discussion
suspension
extension
commission
expansion
concession
compulsion
aggression
impression
impassion
impulsion
submission
expression

concussion
compassion
convulsion
accession
dissension
ascension
expulsion
obsession
percussion
possession
permission
oppression
succession
immersion
dispersion

VCV

o|mis̍|sion
pretension
dimension
emission
profession
repulsion
recession
emulsion
remission

propulsion
secession
revulsion
depression
digression
repression
progression
declension
regression
prehension
recension

__ __ __´sion

apprehension
repercussion
comprehension
supersession
reprehension
prepossession
manumission
condescension
retrogression
intermission
intercession

misapprehension

236

-<u>sion</u> (zhŭn)

vĭ|sion
fusion
version
lesion

ex|pló|sion
conclusion
excursion
confusion
corrosion
occasion
transfusion
perversion
conversion
collision
adhesion
obtrusion
diffusion
allusion
incision
subversion

suffusion
illusion
infusion
incursion
collision

invasion
exclusion
aspersion
intrusion
implosion
inversion
effusion
inclusion
abrasion
contusion
occlusion

de|cí|sion
erosion
reversion
division

profusion
precision
evasion
provision
delusion
derision
cohesion
revision
aversion
elision
prelusion
seclusion
protrusion
preclusion
reclusion

supervision
indecision
subdivision
disillusion
television

Final syllables -ent, -ence*, -ant, -ance*, -ancy, -ency

Spelling aid: Final (ĕns) (ăns) are regularly spelled with c* ence ance

Since these syllables are usually pronounced with the schwa (ŭ) sound, exaggerating the sound of a (ă) and e (ĕ) is often the only spelling aid.

Exaggerate short vowel sounds in final syllables.

parent	stimulant	presence
servant	defendant	instance
student	violent	clearance
rodent	emigrant	essence
serpent	resident	sentence
fragrant	abundant	hindrance
patent	incident	balance
client	dominant	absence

The sound of c or g before -ence and -ance can help to determine spelling.

urgent	recent	pungency
elegant	vacant	diligence
tangent	adjacent	decency
negligent	significant	innocence
arrogant	reticent	magnificence
detergent	applicant	extravagance

Although cy is a suffix for Latin stems, it is rarely added to complete base words. EXCEPTIONS: captaincy bankruptcy
Final (sĭ) in base words is regularly spelled cy.

agency	vacancy	frequency
infancy	urgency	constancy
decency	hesitancy	presidency

*a few words end ense and anse:

dense	intense	dispense	incense
tense	manse	expense	immense
sense	suspense	condense	recompense

-<u>ary</u> (ĕr´i) or (å ri) depending on accent.* (mil´i tĕr´i) (di´å ri)

-<u>ory</u> (ō ri) (ȯ ri) (ter´i tō´ri) (his´tȯ ri)

-<u>ery</u> (ĕr y) is unaccented. (ar chẽr y)

EXCEPTIONS: cem´e tĕr´y   sta´tion ĕr´y   mon´as tĕr´y
             dys´en tĕr´y   con fec´tion ĕr´y   mil´li nĕr´y

Spelling aid: Final (ĕr i) is regularly spelled <u>ary</u>. Note six exceptions above.

-<u>ary</u> (ĕr i)	-<u>ary</u> (å ry)	-<u>ery</u> (ĕr i)
estuary	boundary	flattery
dictionary	glossary	gallery
literary	rosary	scenery
legendary	summary	drapery
commentary	salary	slavery
secretary	burglary	bribery
momentary	documentary	cutlery
February	anniversary	misery
sanctuary	supplementary	trickery
ordinary	**-<u>ory</u> (ō´ri) (ȯ ri)**	drudgery
dignitary	ivory	lottery
mercenary	memory	crockery
honorary	factory	bindery
seminary	rectory	livery
culinary	advisory	shrubbery
centenary	compulsory	refinery
imaginary	auditory	artillery

*Americans and British disagree on the pronunciation of <u>ary</u>. The dictionary shows both. Americans place a secondary accent on <u>ar</u> but pronounce it (ĕr i). British do not accent <u>ar</u>.

<u>library</u>   Amer.: (li brĕr´i) – Brit.: (li´brẽ i)

Amer.: (nes´e sĕr´i) – Brit.: (nes´e sẽr i)

Shifting Accent

A suffix may change the syllable division and/or accent of a base word.
1. Pronounce the base word.
2. Pronounce the base word with the suffix.

magnet - ic   period - ic

metal - ic   idiot - ic

organ - ic   prosper - ity

human - ity   brutal - ity

major - ity   senator - ial

legal - ity   dictator - ial

editor - ial   Boston - ian

adverb - ial   reform - ation

tutor - ial   critic - ism

consult - ation   Catholic - ism

condemn - ation   stupid - ity

parent - al   vital - ity

origin - al   patriot - ic

politic - al   Mason - ic

civil - ian   moment - ous

240

baptism - al

regular - ity

poet - ic

sulphur - ic

rigid - ity

local - ity

synonym - ous

resign - ation

electric - ity

personal - ity

prefer - able

romantic - ism

product - ive

total - ity

frugal - ity

elastic - ity

despot - ic

public - ity

superior - ity

autumn - al

popular - ity

valid - ity

prophet - ic

similar - ity

cynic - ism

mystic - ism

refer - ence

normal - ity

solid - ity

fanatic - ism

prior - ity

rapid - ity

prefer -ence

real - ity

gn	wr	kn
gnarl	wrap	knee
gnash	wrath	knife
gnat	wreak	knit
gnaw	wreck	know
gnome	wren	knot
gnar	wrench	knock
gnu	wrest	knead
	wretch	knelt
feign	wrong	kneel
reign	wring	knight
sign	wrung	knuckle
design	writ	knickers
resign	write	
consign	wry	ps
align	wright	pshaw
assign	writhe	psalm
benign	wraith	pseudo
foreign	wrist	Psalter
mn	wrack	psychic
hymn	wreath	psychology
damn	wrinkle	psychosis
autumn	wrangle	psaltery
column	wrestle	
condemn	wriggle	pt
solemn	written	ptomaine
		receipt

m̶b̶   r̶h̶   t̶

lamb̶   rh̶yme   of̶ten
limb̶   rh̶ythm   lis̶ten
jamb̶   rh̶ubarb   chas̶ten
bomb̶   rh̶inestone chris̶ten
crumb̶   Rh̶esus   Chris̶tmas
dumb̶   rh̶ombus   fas̶ten
numb̶   rh̶omboid   glis̶ten
thumb̶   rh̶apsody   has̶ten
climb̶   rh̶etoric   mois̶ten
comb̶   rh̶eostat   mor̶tgage
          rh̶eumatism
succumb̶   rh̶inoceros

b̶t   g̶h   l̶
deb̶t   gh̶ost   bal̶k
doub̶t   gh̶oul   cal̶k
sub̶tle   gh̶etto   chal̶k
           gh̶erkin   stal̶k
           gh̶astly   tal̶k
h̶   wal̶k
h̶our   fōl̶k
h̶eir   agh̶ast   cal̶f
h̶onor   afgh̶an   hal̶f
h̶onest   sorgh̶um   sal̶ve
Durh̶am   spagh̶etti   sol̶der

243

ear (ûr)

ear is usually pronounced (ēr) as in <u>hear</u>, <u>clear</u>, <u>fear</u>, <u>near</u>, etc. It is pronounced (ûr) in these words:

<u>earth</u>
earthen
earthquake
earthworm
earthly
earthenware
unearthly

<u>early</u>
<u>search</u>
research
searchlight
<u>dearth</u>
<u>rehearse</u>
<u>heard</u>

<u>learn</u>
learned
learnt
unlearned
<u>pearl</u>
<u>yearn</u>
<u>earl</u>

our (ûr)

our is usually pronounced (our) as in <u>our</u>, <u>sour</u>, <u>scour</u>, <u>devour</u>, <u>hour</u>, etc. It is pronounced (ûr) in these words:

<u>journal</u>
journey
sojourn
adjourn
journalist
adjournment
journalism
journeyman
journalistic
<u>scourge</u>
<u>flourish</u>

<u>courage</u>
encourage
discourage
encouragement
discouragement
<u>nourish</u>
undernourish
nourishment
<u>courtesy</u>
courteous
discourteous

Occasionally, final <u>e</u> does not cause a long vowel.

-ine (ĭn)

engine
destine
doctrine
famine
<u>ch</u>lorine
discipline
examine
masculine
feminine
determine
genuine
medicine

<u>i</u> (ē)

sardine
vaccine
r<u>ou</u>tine
Pauline
ma<u>ch</u>ine
police
Bernice
marine
elite
magazine
mezzanine

-<u>ice</u> (ĭs)

office
service
justice
practice
notice
novice
crevice
auspice
jaundice
armistice
apprentice
accomplice
prejudice
cowardice

<u>ite</u> (ĭt)

granite
opposite
favorite
definite
composite
infinite
exquisite
hypocrite
requisite

-<u>ile</u> (ĭl)

missile
fragile
mobile
futile
fusile
hostile

<u>ace</u> (ăs)

surface
Wallace
solace
terrace
preface
menace

purchase
lettuce
college
morale
percale
promise
premise
treatise
privilege
confederate

ture (cho͝or)

capture	furniture
culture	curvature
fracture	indenture
lecture	armature
mixture	overture
nature	aperture
nurture	conjuncture
denture	forfeiture
picture	expenditure
pasture	temperature
gesture	agriculture
posture	legislature
puncture	manufacture
rapture	miniature
rupture	caricature
sculpture	horticulture
texture	
structure	
torture	
vulture	
scripture	
creature	
feature	
future	
fixture	

Pronounce base words,
adding suffix -ure

moist + ure

depart

conject

advent

architect

tu (choo͞)

fortune
statute
statue
virtue
mutual
natural
century
Portugal
punctual
ritual
saturate
spatula
situate
sumptuous
punctuate
fluctuate
actual
impetuous
congratulate
tarantula
infatuate
perpetual
spiritual
habitual
intellectual

i (y)

When <u>i</u> precedes a vowel in final syls, <u>i</u> may be pronounced (y).

<u>Spelling aid</u>: (y) in a final syllable is regularly spelled <u>i</u>.*

i/on or (yŏn)

union
million
stallion
bunion
companion
opinion
rebellion
communion

i/a or (yå)

Asia
Julia
gardenia
magnolia
petunia
Virginia
dahlia

i/an or (yăn)

Asian
Italian
civilization
Brazilian

i/ous or (yŭs)

anxious
noxious
rebellious
obnoxious
ingenious

i/or or (yĕr)

warrior
junior
senior
savior
behavior

i/ar or (yãr)

Spaniard
billiards
familiar
peculiar

- - - - - - -

Daniel
spaniel
genial
congenial
brilliant
valiant
lenient
convenient
William
alien
genius

*Exceptions are (oi) words, spelled <u>oy</u> before vowels:

loyal	voyage	clairvoyant	
royal	foyer	flamboyant	

Also:	canyon	lawyer	halyard	mayor
	beyond	sawyer	lanyard	mayonnaise

Final (sh) Syllables

Just as <u>ti</u> and <u>si</u> combine with <u>on</u> to form the syl. <u>tion</u> and <u>sion</u> (shŭn) ti and si, along with <u>ci</u>, <u>ce</u>, <u>se</u>, may combine with vowels to form other final (sh) syllables.

<u>ti</u>a	<u>ti</u>al	<u>ti</u>ous	<u>ci</u>an	tient	<u>si</u>a
<u>ci</u>a	<u>ci</u>al	<u>ci</u>ous	tian	cient	(zhȧ)
(shȧ)	<u>si</u>al	<u>ce</u>ous	sian	sient	<u>si</u>an
	(shăl)	(shŭs)	(shăn)	(shĕnt)	(zhăn)

All (sh) syls. behave the same:

1. Primary accent falls on syl. before (sh).
2. <u>i</u> before (sh), although accented, will be short – tĭ´tian

facial	gracious	Grecian
racial	luscious	Martian
social	spacious	tertian
glacial	vicious	titian
crucial	conscious	Lucian
martial	specious	gentian
partial	cautious	Dacian
nuptual	tortious	Hessian
spatial	nauseous	
	scrumptious	patience
		conscience
patient	nausea	ratio
transient	Dacia	hoosier
āncient	Asia	species
quotient	Lucia	glacier

248

Final Syls.: (shal) (shus) (shan) (shent) (zha) (zhan), etc.
1. Pronounce final (sh) syl. as one unit. <u>tial</u> (shăl).
2. Remember to accent the syl. before (sh).
3. Remember that only <u>i</u> before (sh) is short. Two exceptions: <u>pre´cious</u> <u>spe´cial</u>

VCCV

official	fictitious	flirtatious
officient	indicia	substantial
officious	efficient	contentious
ambitious	artesian	dissentious
suspicious	tactician	dissentient
essential	mendacious	dissentience
commercial	vexatious	consentient
sufficient	Phoenecian	insentience
optician	audacious	auspicial
infectious	Caucasian	pugnacious
curvaceous	Confucious	technician
mortician	nasturtium	Circassian
omniscient	ambrosia	crustaceous
torrential	auspicious	sententious
Cistercian	magnesia	Helvetia
amnesia	fallacious	pernicious

VCV

initial	physician	vivacious
financial	potential	Parisian
musician	malicious	credential
magician	judicial	ferocious
delicious	judicious	proficient
Venetian	inertia	provincial
Patricia	inertial	precautious

249

Galatians

atrocious

logician

amentia

aphasia

minutia

militia

deficient

Aleutian

nutritious

precocious

sequential

facetious

patrician

palatial

pretentious

licentious

prudential

sagacious

tenacious

capacious

Lawrentian

voracious

fiducial

rapacious

fugacious

propitious

politician

residential

superstitious

circumstantial

Indonesia

presidential

beneficial

superficial

influential

Polynesia

Polynesian

artificial

electrician

repetitious

confidential

obstetrician

sacrificial

expeditious

differential

consequential

coefficient

differentia

ballistician

deferential

equinoctial

preferential

statistician

pertinacious

contumacious

surrepitious

controversial

ostentatious

reverential
rhetorician
prejudicial
avaricious
transferential

Lilliputian
providential
penitential
mathematician
pediatrician

Final <u>ciate</u>, <u>tiate</u> (shĭ āt)

glaciate
satiate
vitiate
appreciate
associate
officiate
excruciate
dissociate
expatiate
ingratiate

insatiate
negotiate
initiate
propitiate
licentiate
depreciate
denunciate
enunciate
emaciate
differentiate

My associate, Hank, denunciates me every Friday. That's when I satiate my need of cash, initiate action, and negotiate for my watch at the pawn shop. My date can't differentiate between what's earned money or isn't, the watch doesn't depreciate by Monday, and I appreciate not knowing what time it is!

251

i̱ (ī) a̱ (å)

Occasionally i̱ and a̱ are long at the end of unaccented syl.

Ī|rene´
idea
ideal
alibi
occupy
multiply
iota
hyena
hydraulic
gigantic
identity
psychology
biography
biology

What is B.W. or companion word?

finality
vitality
priority
ironic
quietus
vibration
migration
librarian
triangular

Latin plurals

fungi
alumni
stimuli

Prefixes di̱, dia̱, bi̱

dioxide
bifocal
biweekly
diagonal
diameter

å|or´|tå

What is B.W. or companion word?

vibrator
fatality
nativity
vacation
c̱haotic
creativity

Prefix a̱ (ā)

amoral
asexual

Final unaccented fy̱ (fī) in 3-or-more syl. words

classify
dignify
fortify
justify
magnify
petrify
signify
terrify
testify
mystify
amplify
certify
mortify
horrify
clarify
glorify
gratify
modify
notify
pacify
purify
qualify
ratify
satisfy

Confusing Words

oyster ouster	interpret interrupt	prohibition probation
bellow below	indigent indignant	physiology psychology
galley gallery	gradation graduation	psychical physical
canopy company	impetus impetuous	retractable retraceable
sinister sister	detonation denotation	deliberate debilitate
perturb protrude	cavity captivity	receptacle respectable
difiant definite	inception inspection	reputation repetition
eligible legible	dentition detention	conservation conversation
compiled complied	precocious precautious	compilation complication
diversion division	dissertation disertion	deposition disposition dispossession

Confusing Words

*through	very	superb	caption
*thought	every	suburb	captain
*thorough	even		
*though	ever	burnet	marital
thorough	very	brunet	martial
through	ever		
thought	even	reverse	viscous
though	every	reserve	viscious
*once	sliver	process	bother
ounce	silver	possess	brother
dose	corny	perverse	patent
*does	crony	preserve	patient
how	ardor	incident	Calvary
*who	adore	indecent	cavalry
sigh	single	banana	impotent
*sign	signal	bandana	important
*lose	bobby	coroner	intimate
loose	booby	corner	imitate
			inanimate
angle	craven	molded	
*angel	cavern	modeled	
			practical
*were	Angelo	carton	particle
*where	Anglo	cartoon	partial

254

Preparation: Recognition of b.w. with its suffix (as opposed to a base word) is essential since the pronunciation and spelling of a b.w. plus suf. is sometimes different from that of a simple b.w.

Spelling: snow´ing as b.w. + suf.
sno´ing as b.w.
Reading: tum b´ld as b.w. + suf.
tum bled as b.w.

Procedures: Concept development from this point continues in Workbook. The remaining pp. to be read are listed below.

Only a few exercises are included for each rule. Continued practice in other workbooks is recommended. Dictations of words, phrases, or sentences should also be given daily.

Exceptions to each rule are listed for presentation ONLY after the student has received much practice with <u>regular</u> spelling.

As each rule is studied, it is suggested that the student copy it on colored paper and place it in the appropriate section of his notebook. He can then put each exercise behind the colored rule sheet to which it pertains.

Remind the student that suffix <u>y</u> is always a vowel.

<u>Sequence of Spelling Rules</u>   WB=Workbook
RSB=Reading Study Book

SUFFIX RULES

Silent <u>e</u>:	WB 97 - 100	
	RSB 257 - 260	Reading final -<u>ble</u>, -<u>dle</u>, -<u>tle</u> + suf. wiggled (wĭg ´ld) NOT (wĭg lĕd)
	WB 101 - 102	Exceptions to rule
1-1-1:	WB 103 - 104	
Silent <u>e</u>	WB 105 - 106	
and 1-1-1	RSB 261	Reading <u>hoping</u>, <u>hopping</u>, etc. Syl. division formulas can be applied to these words. A double con. keeps the V. short. Compare these words to "rabbit" base words in Level I. When dropping final <u>e</u> causes a VCV situation, the first and most common V´CV formula should be used.
2-1-1:	WB 107-108	Since the dictionary allows two spellings for many words, especially those ending in <u>el</u>, <u>jeweler – jeweller</u>, the exercises include root words of <u>mit</u>, <u>pel</u>, and <u>cur</u> and other common-words which MUST follow the rule.

2-1-1:	WB 107 - 108	WARNING: <u>limit</u>, included in the exercise, is accented on first syl. and is not a <u>mit</u> root word!
y:	WB 109 - 110	

Special Reading	RSB 262 - 263	A suf. may change pronunciation of a b.w. <u>origin</u> <u>original</u> Final <u>t</u>, <u>c</u>, and <u>ce</u> combine with suffixes <u>ian</u> and <u>ial</u> to form (shăn) and (shăl)
	RSB 264	Recognizing -<u>ble</u>, -<u>dle</u>, -<u>tle</u> base words with irregularly-added -<u>ity</u> and -<u>ar</u> desirability <u>circular</u>.

PREFIXES: WB 79 - 80

Prefixes may cause double consonants.
Recognizing prefix – b.w. – suffix.
Additional prefix exercises should be given.

PLURAL RULES:

Add <u>s</u>:	WB 111	It was recommended that this be worked in Level I.
Add <u>es</u>:	WB 112	It was recommended that this be worked in Level III.
Final <u>y</u>:	WB 113 - 114 RSB 265	Reading final <u>y</u> b.w. in plural form and with suf. <u>ed</u>. -<u>ied</u> (ĭd) when b.w. ends (ĭ) <u>worried</u> -<u>ied</u> (īd) when b.w. ends (ī) <u>denied</u>
Final <u>f</u>:	WB 115 - 116	
Final <u>o</u>:	WB 117 - 118	
Irregular:	WB 119	
Letters, Figures, and Signs	WB 119 WB 120	All plurals review

POSSESSIVE RULES WB 121 - 124

BASE WORD RULE WB 61
<u>ie</u> - <u>ei</u>

Words ending in silent e drop e before a suffix beginning with a vowel.
In multisyllable words final led is seldom pronounced (lĕd).

Exceptions: misled = prefix and base word
                    bobsled = compound word

What is the base word? fumbled = fumble + ed; bottles = bottle + s.

crippled	bubbles	bugler
ladled	gargles	idleness
rambled	tables	humbly
snuggled	staples	steeples
stifled	trembles	squabbled
ogled	mingles	noodles
jangled	handles	wobbly
guzzled	titles	gentleness
cycled	rumples	doodled
dwindled	rubles	trifles
rippled	oodles	brittleness
twinkled	rumbles	chortled
saddled	sniffles	whittler
gabled	huddles	joggled
circled	Bibles	foibles
quibbled	battles	scruples
babbled	jingles	gurgled
sidled	hobbles	feebleness
swindled	stumbles	sables
raffled	sparkles	nimbleness
bridled	stables	mangled
paddled	hottles	rifles

Small Miracle

who   whose   some   were

I'm Lucy Lee Lacy, I'm ten, and a red head.
I'm baffled by brother who wished I were dead!
He thinks I'm stuck up and my daily notes
     grim.
Well, just let me tell how last month went for
     him!

He scribbled his name with a rock on the wall.
Then tattled that I did it! That isn't all!
He heckled the baby and tussled with Chad
Who tackled him back, then HE sniffled to
     Dad!

He startled the parrot and ruffled the pooches.
He aped sis's date as he gave her some
     smooches!
He scrambled the cards and misplaced all the
     Jacks.
He melted wax candles and smuggled huge
     snacks.

He meddled in attic forbidden and secret,
And crumpled Dad's straw hat and Mom's
    trimmed with egret!
And there's nothing to equal his badness and
    bumbling!
His antics EMBARRASS me – that's why I'm
    grumbling!

Dear Daily Book, really! The month's now
    December.
A miracle's happened I want to remember:
That brother who's eight snuggles up ev'ry
    night
For the story I read him. He thinks that I'm
    bright!

He fondles the poodles, wipes his feet after
    trample.
He washes his freckles. (He sees my example!)
He guzzled his milk, but now drinks like a
    human.
He picks up his puzzle parts, thanks his pal,
    Truman.

He helps collect apples for dumplings and
  cider,
And "sits" Sally Snaggles. (I cannot abide her!)
He cuddles the baby asleep in its cradle,
And mended Dad's tool box and also Mom's
  ladle.

He closes the door so our nerves do not jangle.
And scares off, as a favor, all the boys Sis
  could strangle!
Yes, antics diminish as bells start to jingle.
And, trusting his luck, he just MAY fool Kris
  Kringle!

The Kindergarten Wiggler

Hal wiggles here, he's wiggling there,

He's wiggled past Miss Lee!

He's settling down, he's settled down,

But a SETTLER he'll never be!

Although two <u>r</u>'s in a base word cause the preceding vowel to be short – marry, merry, mirror, borrow – when <u>r</u> has been doubled because of adding a suffix, the base word retains its original sound.

star <u>starry</u> not (stă′ri)   stir stîrring not (stĭr′ring)

What is the base word?

scaring	stilled	robed	hater
scarring	styled	robbed	hatter
starred	snipping	mopping	rated
stared	sniping	moping	ratted
barred	shamming	sloping	scraper
bared	shaming	slopping	scrapper
sparing	tapping	cutter	ridding
sparring	taping	cuter	riding
paring	wadded	biter	canning
parring	waded	bitter	caning
tarish	tilling	tubbing	doting
tarrish	tiling	tubing	dotting
daring	ripper	gaping	dolled
marring	riper	gapping	doled
storing	pining	matting	willed
glary	pinning	mating	wiled
warring	spitting	planing	platted
boring	spiting	planning	plated
cured	stripped	slatted	filling
wiring	striped	slated	filing
jarred	griping	biding	batting
dared	gripping	bidding	bating

A suffix may change the sound of the base word.
Pronounce base word. Then pronounce base word with suffix.

109,110

athlete - ic

divine - ity

melody - ous

confide - ent

adore - ation

colony - al

injury - ous

inspire - ation

execute - ive

recite - ation

remedy - al

preside - ent

microscope - ic

profane - ity

senior - ity

observe - ation

declare - ation

Bible - ical

conductive - ity

industry - ous

reside - ent

indicate - ive

victory - ous

custody - an

admire - able

history - an

oblige - ation

active - ity

telephone - ic

extreme - ity

converse - ation

insane - ity

telescope - ic

expire - ation

sedate - ive

luxury - ous

memory - al

harmony - ous

study - ous

reserve - ation

salute - ation

omnivore - ous

repute - ation

advantage - ous

parasite - ic

serene - ity

perspire - ation

derive - ation

christian - ity

library - an

What happens when t and c combine with -ian and -ial?

music - ian

office - ial

resident - ial

finance - ial

politic - ian

torrent - ial

commerce - ial

magic - ian

confident - ial

tactic - ian

president - ial

logic - ian

province - ial

sacrifice - ial

statistic - ian

clinic - ian

provident - ial

263

ble words do not add ity in the usual manner; the ble becomes bil before ity and is always accented.

Discuss orally.

Add ity:

desirable _desirability_

legible _____

noble _____

probable _____

responsible _____

reliable _____

able _____

What is the base word?

stability _stable___

durability _____

eligibility _____

feasibility _____

visibility _____

liability _____

flexibility _____

What is the -ble, -dle, -tle, etc. companion word?

circular _circle_____

singular _____

rectangular _____

angular _____

muscular _____

triangular _____

particular _____

Make adjectives:

spectacle _spectacular_

vehicle _____

oracle _____

quadrangle _____

ventricle _____

tubercle _____

corpuscle _____

113,114

Words ending in y after a consonant change y to i before a suffix unless suffix begins with i. fry = fried but frying

Words ending in y after a consonant form plurals – and third person singular verbs – by changing y to i and adding es. lady – ladies but boy – boys. I fry, but he, she, and it fries.

What is the base word?

hurried = hurry + ed (hur´id)	dried = dry + ed (drīd)	Find two suffixes. Each suffix is applied regularly.
worried	died	fussiness
emptied	spied	noisily
envied	pried	roomiest
copied	tried	cloudier
pitied	defied	moodiness
studied	denied	worldliness
married	relied	oiliness
carried	replied	sleepiest
jellied	implied	stuffiness
candied	satisfied	slimiest
ferried	occupied	lousiness
rallied	pacified	livelihood
		dressiest
buggies	classifies	stickiness
cities	purifies	showiest
bellies	dignifies	thorniest
bunnies	qualifies	worthiness
armies	certifies	jerkily
berries	gratifies	gustiness